IMAGES
of America

'SCONSET

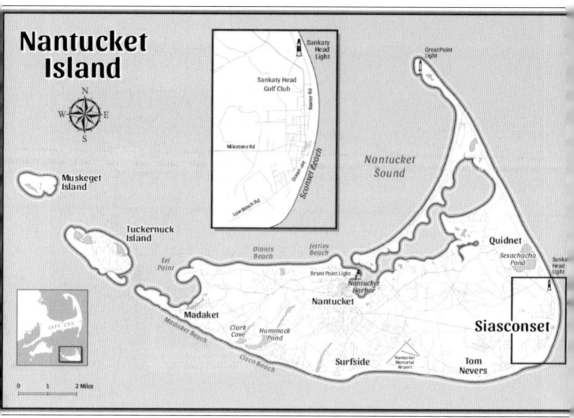

Nantucket Island

N W E S

Muskeget Island

Tuckernuck Island

Eel Point

Sankaty Head Light

Sankaty Head Golf Club

Baxter Rd

Milestone Rd

'Sconset Beach

Ocean Ave

Low Beach Rd

Great Point Light

Nantucket Sound

Dionis Beach

Jetties Beach

Quidnet

Sesachacha Pond

Sankaty Head Light

Brant Point Light

Nantucket Harbor

Nantucket

Madaket

Madaket Beach

Clark Cove

Hummock Pond

Cisco Beach

Surfside

Nantucket Memorial Airport

Siasconset

Tom Nevers

CAPE COD

0   1   2 Miles

This map of today's Nantucket, designed by cartographer Michael Trust, pinpoints the location of Siasconset (popularly referred to as 'Sconset) in the southeastern corner of the Massachusetts island and other major villages and landmarks across the Grey Lady. Nantucket lies 30 miles south of Cape Cod and seven and a quarter miles east of Martha's Vineyard. (Courtesy of Michael Trust.)

ON THE COVER: Little Annie Alden Folger holds the pump handle in this 1890s photograph of Pump Square by Henry S. Wyer. Joe Norcross is behind the pump, while the other boy is unidentified. The c. 1790 house is known as "the Corners," located at the convergence of Shell, Center, and New Streets and is owned today by Mary O'Connell. (Courtesy of the Nantucket Historical Association.)

IMAGES
of America
'SCONSET

Rob Benchley and Richard Trust

ARCADIA
PUBLISHING

Published by Arcadia Publishing
Charleston, South Carolina

Printed in the United States of America

Library of Congress Control Number: 2019947440

For all general information, please contact Arcadia Publishing:
Telephone 843-853-2070
Fax 843-853-0044
E-mail sales@arcadiapublishing.com
For customer service and orders:
Toll-Free 1-888-313-2665

Visit us on the Internet at www.arcadiapublishing.com

A dedication would not be complete without remembering those who paid attention very long ago in their everyday business. For my part, these pages are dedicated to the journalists, essayists, columnists, and photographers of a century (and more!) ago who took the time to take note, even if it was the drudgery of the day. Every word and photograph contributes to this book. Here's to all of the storytellers.

—Rob Benchley

To a special village: All is well now. We've found our place in the universe. We've found 'Sconset.

—Richard Trust

CONTENTS

ACKNOWLEDGMENTS

Hand-in-hand appreciation goes out to two stellar institutions in our Nantucket community: the Nantucket Historical Association (NHA) and the Atheneum Library. The NHA Research Library provided nearly all of the historical photographs in this little book from its vast collection of images so carefully cataloged and archived; our sincerest thanks are given to archives specialist Marie "Ralph" Henke and Amelia Holmes, the library's associate director. Their knowledge, support, and patience were essential in putting this volume in your hands. All photographs in this book are courtesy of the NHA, unless noted. A parallel schooner full of thanks is also given to the people of the Nantucket Atheneum Library, whose digital historical newspaper archive was indispensable in providing voice, context, and confidence in our captions.

And great mention is due to the mother ship Arcadia Publishing, whose Images of America series enables ordinary people the means to chronicle their favorite Main Streets. A warm nod to Caitrin Cunningham, Arcadia senior title manager, whose thoughtful tone and encouraging words kept us on course. To Bob Felch, our unmitigated gratitude for his keen insight and advice as our text morphed from skeletal fragments to a full body of work. DeWitt Smith's 11th-hour contributions were timely enough to add more depth and texture to the project.

Admiration for, and heartfelt thanks to, Dr. Adam Zucker, Matt Johannesen, Dan Tasker, Capt. Mark Donovan, a woman named Melon, and another named Pooch. Really. You know why you are here.

Applause goes to 'Sconset natives Bevin Bixby and Nelson "Snooky" Eldridge, both still savoring the village life. A serendipitous meeting with Lauren Sleeth led us to Ms. Bixby during the planning stages of our writing. These pages would have been less significant without Bevin's inclusion and contribution. Thank you, Lauren. Thank you, Bevin. Mark Donato, Alex Ulgenalp, and Cindy and Rolf Nelson all arrived on Nantucket as "wash-ashores" but became part of the 'Sconset fabric. Finally, a note of respect for, and recognition of, the legacy of the Folger family, whose ancestral thread dates to the founding fathers and their pioneer spirit in the creation of an island society and, ultimately, a village unlike any other anywhere else. To Sheila Folger Todd and Sally Folger Lamott, much gratitude for providing valuable shards of history, both spoken with assured authority and material photographic. Their brother Walter Folger was interviewed for this book three months before he passed away in September 2017 at age 93. A World War II Merchant Mariner and later a US Coast Guardsman who rose to the rank of captain, he spoke glowingly of his native 'Sconset. His granddaughter Victoria Pardo was among those who watched over Walter in his final days. Victoria has spent many summers and many parts of other seasons in 'Sconset and, having studied architecture, historic preservation, and the like in graduate school, she has a clear vision of what it takes to preserve a village such as 'Sconset. Apparently, it also takes a village to write about one.

INTRODUCTION

As the oft-told tale goes, two women are in the airport ticket line in Athens, Greece. One notices a Nantucket lightship basket on the arm of the other. Tapping the basket owner on the shoulder, she says, "I couldn't help noticing that you're from Nantucket. So am I." To which the other responds, "Heavens, no, my dear. I am from 'Sconset!"

Such a sentiment indicates how special it is for those who treasure Siasconset—the enchanted little village, known more commonly as 'Sconset, on the southeastern shore of Nantucket Island.

Whether first-time visitors, summer residents, or the rare breed of year-round 'Sconseters, the tie that binds lovers of the village is not apt to be broken. It is likely to be a life-long romance, rekindled each time one heads back down Milestone Road after some time away and spots that tunnel of trees leading to the Main Street rotary and reentry into the magic kingdom.

Ah, yes, breathe in the air. Home again.

Indeed, more than a few folks visiting for the first time have been moved to exclaim, "I feel like I'm home."

'Sconset is home to an average of 200 year-rounders and swells to 2,000 or more during summer. In the 1700s, approximately 30 or 40 houses dotted the little hamlet. By 1973, some 600 homes were in place. When the year 2000 rolled around, more than 800 families had set up housekeeping; most of those houses were unoccupied during the winter.

What is 'Sconset like in winter months? "It's quiet," year-round resident Dave Dunn says. "There aren't many people out here in 'Sconset. I could stand in the middle of Main Street and not see anybody for an hour. It's wild. You see all these houses with the lights off. In the summertime, all these houses are full of life."

The only 'Sconset "business" open in winter is the post office. Every day at 10:00 a.m., Dunn visits postal clerk Georgia Fowler and picks up his mail. The post office is a central meeting spot in summer as residents and renters alike stop not only to gather up their letters and packages but to chat and renew acquaintances after a lengthy offseason away. In summer, there is much chatter. In winter, not so much.

A Wampanoag Algonquian word for "place of great bones," Siasconset is the only island village outside of Nantucket town with its own zip code (02564). In season are four restaurants and a market as a purveyor of groceries and a whole lot more. The sports appetite is satisfied by 11 tennis courts at the Siasconset Casino and a trio of golf courses.

About 3,000 members of the Wampanoag tribe inhabited the island when they met with a group of English settlers in 1659. In 1686, Jethro Coffin married Mary Gardner on land given to them by his father, Peter, and with lumber from her father, John, they built a Sunset Hill home that today is known as "the Oldest House."

Many of the early settlers made their livelihood fishing near the shores. Cod was plentiful, and eventually, many men were drawn to the best fishing spots on the remote eastern end of the island. By the 1670s, Siasconset was one of four fishing "stands," or stations, where fishermen lived during the spring and fall cod-fishing seasons. The fishermen built small cottages to accommodate the five-man fishing crews. But those were not the charming cottages you see today. Rather, they were little more than one-room wooden shacks with shingled roofs and dirt floors. Cooking was done in the open air or on open porches.

Eventually, a settlement at neighboring Sesachacha was abandoned, and many of its shanties were moved to 'Sconset, which began to take on the appearance of a small village. Many of the seasonal fishermen decided to make 'Sconset their permanent home and began expanding their tiny dwellings to provide year-round shelter for their families. Rather than demolish the shacks and start from scratch, additions were made using odds and ends, including old doors and windows, and sometimes parts of wrecked ships. Many of the fishing shanties transformed into cozy cottages, with their add-ons known as "warts," still stand. Most visitors would never guess that today's endearing, rose-covered cottages started out as earthy fishing shacks. By the early 1800s, 'Sconset had become a popular summer resort for islanders who lived in town. Land in 'Sconset that was first visited by non-Native Americans late in the 17th century in the pursuit of fishing and whaling now caters to the tourist trade. And tourists love their automobiles, which were not allowed on Nantucket until 1918. Cars crowd the roads during the busy summertime, yet Nantucket remains an island with not a single traffic light.

Those who have absorbed the essence of 'Sconset, and reveled in what they love about it, cannot expunge it from their systems—nor do they want to. The late Suzanne DeHeart (1934–2016), of the family of the Wade Cottages, was brought to 'Sconset as a one-year-old in 1935. By that account, she was almost a native. She never took the village for granted and appreciated everything about it. "I make myself go off-island just for the sheer pleasure of coming home," she told Nancy Anne Newhouse in an interview for the 2004 publication, *Voices of the Village: An oral history of 'Sconset*. Suzanne left no doubt about her romancing the hamlet of the 02564 zip code: "If I didn't live here, I'd go find someplace that looked like this and live there, so I might as well stay here."

The lure of 'Sconset is to some the cool breezes and the scent of sea and sand and spray where the waves crash and crawl to the shore, from Low Beach on the southern reach to blankets and umbrellas camped just outside the Summer House, up through the dune grasses of Codfish Park all the way north to the bluff below from where Sankaty Head Lighthouse was moved.

To some, it is a frequent veil of fog that envelops the village in a dewy shroud. To many others, it is the rose-covered cottages or the quiet lanes and paths that meander past those oft-photographed dwellings. To some, it is the way hydrangeas grow with an uncommon lushness, the result of perfect soil and pure 'Sconset air tinged with just the right fraction of moisture. It can be the sweet, unmistakable waft of beach roses. It can be the Siasconset Casino, a lovely edifice opened in 1900, where its clay courts are populated by players in their mandatory whites, and the public may play at certain times each day.

Maybe it is the Siasconset Union Chapel. Dating to 1883, the chapel is a major focal point and gathering place throughout the summer months for religious services and weddings but also is a center for community gatherings for lectures, musical entertainment (typically classical), picnics, and games.

Perhaps it is the wacky or whimsical names on cottage quarterboards: "Seldom Inn," "Gone Crazy," "Hedged About," "Svargaloka," "the Sheiling," "La Petite Cottage," and what might top them all, "Wanackmamack."

'Sconset is made for slow, carefree walks with drippy ice-cream cones past perfectly groomed privet hedges, many of the latter towering over flowered gardens. It is made for slow walks across the Gully Footbridge, where when you look one way, you gaze upon the beach; look in another direction, it is the sundial on the side of a house; look down, and it is a healthy row of hydrangeas.

'Sconset is in vast contrast to the bustle of busy Nantucket town, seven miles away—and with a wholly different state of mind. You will like (or love) 'Sconset if you like quaint, if you like quiet. Hydrangeas do not make a sound.

When the initial trickle of European settlers reached Nantucket in 1659, the residing Native Americans had already been fishing off Siasconset. By the late 1700s, 'Sconset had become a pleasant diversion for those Nantucket town residents needing a summer break. The opening of the Atlantic House hotel on Main Street in 'Sconset in 1848 helped feed the move to tourism. After the Civil War ended in 1865, with the economy booming, people from off-island began trekking to 'Sconset in greater numbers. Nantucket's railroad service to 'Sconset began in 1884, offering more visitors the opportunity for a Siasconset vacation.

Such holiday getaways had taken a quantum leap with the construction of cottages, during much of the 1880s, by Edward F. Underhill, among others, and the influx of actors who fled non-air-conditioned theaters in 1890s Boston and New York City summers. The Actors Colony became part of 'Sconset history.

Yet for all its allure, 'Sconset is a fragile outpost. Beach and bluff erosion threaten the very land itself. In 1841 and again in the 1990s, storms and erosion destroyed cottages in the Codfish Park neighborhood. In 2007, the iconic red and white Sankaty Head Lighthouse—which flashed its first signals in 1850—was moved to a spot 267 feet inland, near the fifth hole of Sankaty Head Golf Club, to keep it safe from toppling into the sea below what was its eroding, bluff-side setting.

Over-development is always a concern of those who cherish 'Sconset and its place in history, but the citizenry has friends who strive to curb the disappearance of precious landscape. Such organizations as the Nantucket Islands Land Bank and the 'Sconset Trust have saved acres upon acres from the hammers and nails of home construction, aka village destruction.

"I think 'Sconset has maintained the same charm it had when I arrived here in 1980," said Mark Donato, who ran the 'Sconset Market for 36 summers. "It looks the same and it feels the same. The new people moving in, the new 'Sconseters, have the best intentions and love it for what it is, and strive to keep it what it is. I'm not the least bit worried about the future. I see all good things."

President emeritus of the Siasconset Civic League after completing two three-year terms as its head, Donato said the work that was done to hold off erosion in Codfish Park has been a success story.

"I believe we are winning that game, and I think that modern engineering and science work," said Donato. "It's a tried and proven record they have on their side, and I believe we are going to save the bluff in perpetuity.

"I owned a house in Codfish Park, and water was lapping at my door. I sold, and now Codfish Park is rock solid. It has been for several years."

Many nonprofit organizations are in place to protect the interests of 'Sconset. The 'Sconset Trust is a major nonprofit, its mission multidirectional, to wit "dedicated to the conservation of moors, beaches, marshlands, and meadows in a wild state; the preservation of buildings and sites of historic significance; the protection of areas of natural beauty; the safeguarding of the public water supply; and the production of educational materials about 'Sconset's social, economic, and natural history."

Among other groups predicated on keeping 'Sconset free of compromising its essence architecturally, culturally, and socially are the Siasconset Beach Preservation Fund, 'Sconset Advisory Board, Siasconset Civic Association, Siasconset Historical Research Group, and Nantucket Preservation Trust.

They take great care of this special place in the universe. It is special, to be sure, and please, take great care not to call it simply Nantucket. Heavens, no. It is 'Sconset.

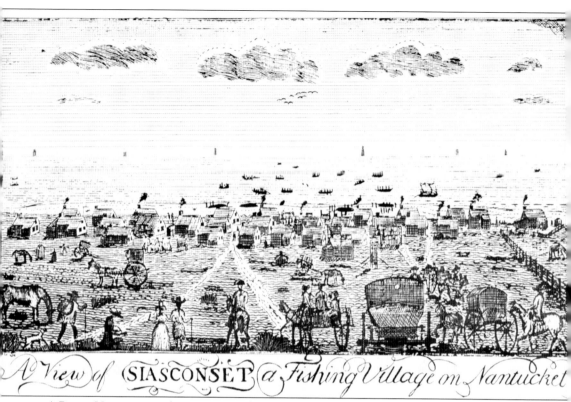

A View of SIASCONSET a Fishing Village on Nantucket

A Brown University graduate, artist, and writer, David Augustus Leonard provided the first image of 'Sconset with this engraved pictorial titled "A View of Siasconset a Fishing Village on Nantucket, 1797." Leonard (1771–1818) portrays 'Sconset as having a prosperous cod fishing community, whose residents sheltered themselves in simple, Old World–style houses. Also pictured are box carts and horse carriages and the people who drove them. Leonard is said to have resided on Nantucket for an unspecified period while working as a schoolteacher. Moreover, he wrote "Laws of Siasconset: A Ballad," which, in part, offers, "Siasconset is a pleasant village . . . erected by Gentlemen in town for their temporary convenience, during the season of fishing, which happens twice a year, Spring and Autumn. . . . It is much frequented, not only by those who are employed in fishing but also by a great number of visitants who afford themselves . . . much festivity, and true sociability."

One

In the Beginning

The foundation of Nantucket Island is a massif of boulders, sand, and clay from the tailings of the last continental glacier. The geologists call it a "terminal moraine," and it is part of a vast, 5,800-mile earthen chain that snakes its way from St. John's, Newfoundland, to the Beaufort Sea in the Canadian Yukon—seven time zones away. About 21,000 years ago, sandy beaches, plains, and bays began forming as the sea level rose, stranding this proto-island in the flashing sea. Thus was the beginning of the place known as "Siasconset," perched on the island's southeastern shore, with 3,000 miles of unobstructed ocean between it and the coast of Spain; it was then a treeless prairie, and today, it remains beaten about the face and body by three-day nor'easters.

The Wampanoag, who identify themselves as the People of the First Light, were Siasconset's original residents, its first fishermen, and the composers of its name. Indeed, the first light of the current millennium fell on this very shore. In time, Siasconset's first syllables were nipped off, and it became simply 'Sconset. The laws of 'Sconset dictate that the use of the apostrophe is mandatory. Like a magic charm on a wizard's pendant, it is just not 'Sconset without it.

Although it became a renowned summer resort in the mid- to late 1800s, it has always been home to a sturdy throng of the self-sufficient who still spend the off-season leaning against the wind. Also, 'Sconseters live under the great Atlantic migratory flyway, so it is inevitable that an Odd Duck or two falls out of the sky from time to time to take roost here for good. Before the time when the ancient fishing cottages became covered in roses, before the palmy days of melting ice-cream cones, mile-high privet hedges, tennis courts, and swimming pools, old 'Sconset was an expanse of wild and dusty rawness—the trees, roses and shell streets came much later. Yet today, one needs only to walk a short distance from the oasis to see unrefined chaos at work, where nature battles itself, and people are mere flecks upon it. Herman Melville reflected further during a visit to Sankaty Head Lighthouse in 1852. Writing to his friend Nathaniel Hawthorne about a story idea, he reported warily about the state of the sea 100 feet below the bluff: "Here, in strange & beautiful contrast, we have the innocence of the land placidly eyeing the malignity of the sea."

Looking northward, most likely on Front Street, fishermen's shacks were built mostly from lumber scavenged from other buildings and driftwood. These fishing huts were built up on the bank near 'Sconset's shoreline, where the cod were plentiful. Through the years, these unassuming shacks became much improved, creating the "bones" of the houses that would become the vintage homes seen today.

In this view of Broadway, also in the heart of the village, a group of children posed for the camera in front of more "whale houses," as they were also known. When this photograph was taken in the 1870s, photography was relatively new to the country; glass negatives were used in cameras mounted on tripods and required long exposures—people needed to sit still while the photograph was taken. (Photograph by Josiah Freeman, courtesy of the New York Public Library.)

Horse-drawn carriages and well-dressed 'Sconseters stood very still while the cameraman took this photograph at the bottom of Main Street in the 1860s. Improved roadways were a thing of the future then, which, after the rain, made any kind of travel challenging. The house pictured at the center would become the site of the 'Sconset Market. This view looks eastward over the Atlantic.

This wagon is known as a 'Sconset Fish Dray. In the days of four-hoofed-drive, when the village's notoriety for codfish was at its peak, fishermen hauled their catch up from the beach in this modified wheel-barrow. The boys pictured, along Front Street, were probably not those same fishermen, but the drays became props in the images of the commercial photographers of the time—in this case, 1882.

A Nantucket-designed fishing dory is part of the scene amidst shanties on Front Street in 1869. Those who posed for the photographer include Caroline Parker (at center, wearing a headscarf) whose first husband left her and her children for gold in California in 1849; he died along the way in Chile from yellow fever. Such are the stories from 'Sconset.

"Shanunga" is the name of this Broadway house, named after the 1852 wreck of a ship by the same name. The original wing of the house is thought to have been built in the late 1600s. It became the "unofficial" post office in 1872, and its "unofficial" deliveryman was Capt. William Baxter, who can be seen here at the reins of his wagon, although his horse seems to be elsewhere.

Horse-drawn carriages with drivers and passengers gather at the hub of 'Sconset known as "the Square" in 1905. At the center of the photograph is the "new" post office, flanked on the right by the Siasconset Bookstore. The latter is now a small seasonal restaurant called the 'Sconset Café, adjoined by a liquor store called, curiously enough, the 'Sconset Bookstore.

Anna E.C. Barrett was the 'Sconset postmistress from 1897 until 1928. Here, she stands in the doorway of the current post office, which was acquired in 1902. Open all year long, it continues to be a community nexus of ideas, information, and social solidarity. Except for a 10-year period beginning in 1874, 'Sconset has had its post office for almost 150 years.

As the fish stocks declined and the tourism increased, bringing grand hotels and many new summer homes to 'Sconset, commercial photography gained a footing. The mix of the fishing relics and many more visitors created inviting opportunities for anyone with the proper equipment. Here, an old dory makes the perfect setting for an 1880s family portrait. The location is along Ocean Avenue, looking eastward over the village's broad sand flats.

A SIASCONSET COTTAGE.

Originally named "Tuckernook," this 'Sconset whale house (which was later renamed "Bigenough") was largely destroyed when it was converted into a garage serving the house next door. The house next door, described in one architectural commentary as a "Victorian monstrosity," replaced an original fish house ("the Woodbine"), which was moved across town in 1884 to make room for the bigger house that still stands today. Ironically, the latter house was named "Too Big."

There are a number of ancient houses in 'Sconset, including Shanunga (page 15), and here, "Auld Lang Syne," which is reputed by 'Sconseters to be the oldest house on Nantucket. Period. Derived from the original 17th-century fish houses, Shanunga was built in the 1680s, and Auld Lang Syne in 1675. All were built as simple rectangles with earthen floors; in the following years, small additions were added, known as "warts." They have survived the centuries.

The other "Oldest House" on the island is also known as the Jethro Coffin House. Built in 1686 on a hill west of downtown Nantucket, it was a wedding gift for Jethro Coffin (1663–1727) and Mary Gardner (1670–1767). Playful debate still exists about who claims the oldest house on Nantucket. In the far background is the 1886 Sea Cliff Inn, built by Charles Robinson, who developed much of 'Sconset during that period. (Courtesy of Rob Benchley, a gift of Marie Giffin, the *Inquirer and Mirror*.)

Harry Dunham was one of many farmers on Nantucket who delivered milk and vegetables to customers in 'Sconset. Dunham, whose Greenwood Farm went right down to the shoreline at Polpis Harbor, was part of the important legacy of farming on Nantucket after the decline of whaling. In the 1860s, there were more than 100 active farms on the island; 20 of them were in little old 'Sconset.

In the 1920s, this former livery stable was converted into an inn known as the Tavern on the Moors. It became the home of the 'Sconset School of Opinion, the brainchild of Ohio senator Frederic C. Howe. Summer lectures and other forms of entertainment were offered there, but not without controversy. "We don't want this sort of thing here, and we don't intend to have it," one writer complained to the *Inquirer and Mirror* newspaper. "We believe that Mr. Howe is trying to set up a sort of Socialist Chautauqua on the island."

In addition to building the Ocean View House hotel (1873) and the 'Sconset Union Chapel (1883), Charles Robinson built this picturesque wooden footbridge across the gully road separating the old village (above) to the north, with his new "village" of Victorian cottages to the south. It became an essential pedestrian thoroughfare, spanning the road to the public beach, and remains a scenic overlook for photographers, bird-watching, sunrises, and an occasional marriage proposal.

"Below bank" is still used to describe this area of 'Sconset, which would later become known as Codfish Park. At the easternmost edge of the village, its once-bountiful supply of cod was wholly responsible for the creation of the settlement in the 1600s. In this 1885 photograph, folks gathered en masse for a community "Squantum," a public beach picnic where fresh codfish was at the top of the menu. At the time, salesmen advertised 'Sconset's aura as an "elixir for the world's woes."

The Massachusetts Highway Commission was created in 1892, making public funds available for roadway engineering and construction statewide. Nantucket wasted no time in applying to the commission for assistance, and by 1894, the Milestone Road, linking town with 'Sconset, was underway. The six-and-a-half-mile stretch took years to complete, but it was far better than the previous track, which was a knee-deep rutted nightmare from generations of horse-and-buggy use.

The island's board of selectmen banned the use of automobiles and motorcycles "from all the highways of the town of Nantucket" in 1906, a bylaw that split the community pretty much down the middle. But Clinton Folger found a way to get the US mail to 'Sconset expeditiously by towing his Overland through the streets to the (state-owned) Milestone Road, where the town had no jurisdiction. The law was repealed in 1918, and the autos streamed in: 273 cars in 1922 and tens of thousands today—and still not a traffic light on the island.

Nantucket-born Henry S. Wyer (1847–1920) was a prolific Island photographer, and he was no stranger to 'Sconset. On this summer day in the 1880s, his camera caught a southwards view of the North Bluff as its development was growing towards Sankaty Head Lighthouse. Note the wide, grass-covered sand flats on the left. This beach feature has all but disappeared due to 20th-century erosion.

The mansard-roofed house "Flaggship" was so-named after William J. Flagg, an 1870s developer who bought much of the expansive sheep-pastureland north of the village all the way up to Sankaty Head Lighthouse. This northward expansion of 'Sconset seems to have been welcomed, since after his death in 1898, people were concerned that his heirs had not "finished" his work. But his unforgotten legacy is a public footpath he created (crossing everyone's front yards) that winds its way from the village up to a point just short of where the lighthouse stood until its 2007 move safely inland.

This 1920s aerial view of 'Sconset's North Bluff shows summer homes along Baxter Road, which were built around the turn of the 20th century. Flagg's house (seen in the photograph on the previous page), can be located at the far left. As for the houses, not too much has changed in the past 100 years; as for the vegetated bluff in the foreground, much of it is gone or endangered because of erosion.

Sankaty Head Lighthouse was built in 1850 at the north end of Baxter Road (see Chapter 6). In this 1961 aerial photograph, the end of Flagg's footpath can be seen at the lower right, but because of relentless erosion, much of this land has vanished. The upper and lower houses pictured in the foreground have been moved, and the house in the middle went up in smoke in 1977. (Photograph by Nathaniel G. Benchley, courtesy of Rob Benchley.)

The landscape is harsh and barren in this 1870s view of the footbridge over Gully Road, which leads to 'Sconset's famous bathing beach. But what was once a coastal prairie has become a tree-lined, vegetated village, full of rose-covered cottages, tennis courts, lawn sprinklers, and an ice-cream parlor. It is also the place where generations of hardy year-rounders call home. Here, they lean against the wind.

WHY WORRY!
"I am an old man, and have had many troubles,
but most of 'em never happened."

William "Billy" Bowen was a self-made 'Sconset sage whose face and salty wisdom appeared many times in the *Inquirer and Mirror* newspaper and in other publications. In this postcard reproduction, he asks a question and aptly answers it: "Why Worry?" Wearing a Sou'wester and smoking a pipe, he states that "I am an old man, and have had many troubles, but most of 'em never happened." (Courtesy of Rob Benchley.)

Two

VILLAGE VISITORS

The transition from undefined, unremarkable, practically undesirable land seven miles southeast of Nantucket town to highly praised, highly prized residential and vacation property on ocean's edge began with a trickle in the 18th century and escalated rapidly at the end of the 19th century and beginning of the 20th. That is 'Sconset.

What once featured seasonal fishing and whaling in the early to mid-1800s was a village evolving. Bare-boned, one-story, dirt-floor fishing shanties marked the 'Sconset architectural "style" when the initial visitors from town traversed by horse-drawn wagons the unpaved, uneven, uncomfortably rutted thoroughfare that today is a comfortable Milestone Road—a smooth, straight shot, with some undulation—to Siasconset.

Those little fishing shacks gave way to new and bigger homes that would alter the face and fabric of 'Sconset and stamp the tiny village as a summer resort of unparalleled appeal, right into, eventually, the 21st century. Builders in the late 1800s, including Charles H. Robinson, William J. Flagg, and Edward F. Underhill, developed homes and hotels that drew flocks of tourists.

Among the influx of summer pleasure-seekers were actors and actresses from Boston and New York City. Off-stage for the hot summers because the big-city theaters had no air conditioning, many of the day's leading performers trekked to 'Sconset for the relaxing, rejuvenating salt air and breezes, the ocean waters, and the cottages of Robinson, Flagg, and Underhill. Thus was collectively formed the Actors Colony. Annually drinking from the fountain of restorative juices, some kings and queens of the stage either rented homes for June, July, and August or bought houses outright.

A post office, golf courses, the Union Chapel, the casino, and businesses offering various goods and services led 'Sconset into the 20th century. A narrow-gauge railroad led townies and off-islanders into 'Sconset from 1884 to 1917.

Then the horseless carriage—otherwise known as the automobile—was allowed on the roads of Nantucket in 1918. And when motion pictures—otherwise known as the movies—became significant and standard fare in Hollywood, many stage actors heard the call and left the East Coast in favor of the west. With the advent of air conditioning in Broadway theaters, the acting corps, to a large degree, spent subsequent summers in New York City. By 1925, the Actors Colony would essentially be gone but surely not forgotten.

Visitors are drawn to the rose-covered cottages of 'Sconset—such as *Barque* on Ocean Avenue (above) and *In and Out* in Pump Square (below)—but it was not until early in the 20th century that the tradition became firmly rooted. Florence Hill, a landscape architect familiar with Nantucket's moist climate and sandy soil essential for growing healthy roses, was the visionary who set the tone. As posted in a July 1959 'Sconset Notes column in the Nantucket newspaper *Inquirer and Mirror,* Hill's profession enabled her to buy rose bushes wholesale and at a quantity discount. Initially, she bought 1,000 bushes for 22¢ each and sold them all at cost. With the new look exciting homeowners, in subsequent years, Hill purchased 1,500 more bushes. Today, roses of various colors and varieties climb and cover cottage fences and houses throughout the village. 'Sconset would not be 'Sconset without the roses—nor would it be without Florence Hill. (Both photographs by Richard Trust.)

Rose-covered cottages are frequent subjects of artists, and the boy pictured here grew up and became quite accomplished with brush and paint. The boy—age five when photographed in 1924—is Robert Benchley Jr., who would make his living in the advertising business and is the late father of this book's coauthor, Rob Benchley. The watercolor of a rose-covered cottage on Lily Street shown here is by Benchley Jr. (Both, courtesy of Rob Benchley.)

The transformation of the Atlantic House at 27 Main Street from hotel to private residence, shown here, was led by renowned architect Frederick P. Hill. The property at the time of conversion, in the 1920s, was owned by noted philanthropist David Gray. Gray was the high bidder in a public auction held after the previous owner was forced to sell the hotel for failure to pay the taxes. Repositioned on its lot of land by Hill during his overhaul, 27 Main has remained in private hands. (Photograph by Rob Benchley.)

The year was 1848 when the Atlantic House, above, opened at 27 Main Street as 'Sconset's first hotel. Twenty-seven partners had bought the land upon which construction took place, giving the village a strong base on its way to becoming a full-scale player in the tourist trade that is the backbone of the island's economy today. The building, pictured here in 1910, was in business as a hotel until the 1920s when it was downsized and otherwise reconfigured as a private residence.

The Beach House hotel, pictured here on a postcard postmarked 1951, was on the South Bluff's Ocean Avenue between Pochick and Carew Streets. It was opened in 1901 under innkeeper G. Herbert Brinton, offering an unobstructed view of 'Sconset Beach and the Atlantic Ocean, and as it faced east, gorgeous sunrises were enjoyed from any spot on the expansive venue. The Beach House was closed and subsequently demolished in 1957.

Three young men enjoying a day bathing in the surf and soaking up the sun on 'Sconset Beach early in the 20th century are clowning for the camera. Note their headbands and bows.

Local builder Charles H. Robinson and partner Dr. Franklin A. Ellis built the Ocean View House, a hotel that opened in 'Sconset in 1873 and checked in its last guest before it was torn down in 1919. In October 1883, Robinson added the annex to the Ocean View House across the road from the original buildings.

Guests arriving at the Ocean View House after having taken the train to 'Sconset were greeted by hotel owner Doc Powers and his blowing a bugle while atop a donkey in front of the Siasconset Bookstore and post office. Powers would reprise his performance when his guests departed.

A Civil War correspondent for the New York Times (among other modes of employment and ventures) and once jailed by the Confederacy even after his acquittal on charges of spying for the Union, Edward F. Underhill turned to building and developed a 'Sconset neighborhood on land purchased south of the village in 1879. Constructing almost two dozen cottages based on the original fishermen's shacks, or shanties, Underhill (1830–1898) described the old houses as "all squatty, one-story affairs, no two alike. . . . Lots of new cottages built in the old style. Latch strings on doors. Quaint ornamentation."

China Closet is the name of the cottage where, during the summer months, Edward and Evelyn Underhill lived and displayed in their home on Pochick at Ocean Avenue their vast collection of china and other items acquired during their world travels. After Edward died, Evelyn, according to Nantucket Historical Association archives, "gave a home to a young black woman and her daughter, Florence Higginbotham. When Evelyn was in her 80s and having lost her fortune . . . Florence gave Evelyn, and her china, a home at her house [in town] at 27 York Street."

A woman is seated and two men are standing on the front porch of this Underhill cottage on Evelyn Street in 'Sconset. Named in honor of Edward F. Underhill's wife, Evelyn, the street was nothing more than a dirt track through low grass at that point late in the 19th century.

This is Lily Street, pictured as one of three streets lined with Underhill cottages: Lily Street, named for his daughter; Evelyn Street, named for his wife; and Pochick Street, named for Pochick Rip, located off the 'Sconset shore.

'Sconset home builder and developer Charles H. Robinson's image is captured by an unknown photographer at age 80 in 1909. Robinson and his associate, Franklin A. Ellis, laid out Ocean Avenue. Pictured here in an overcoat with hat and gloves, Robinson (1829–1915) also was president of the Wannacomet Water Company.

A classic example of Victorian Gothic Revival architecture favored by builder/developer Charles H. Robinson and his partner, Franklin A. Ellis (1833–1884), is the Wolf's Head cottage, now settled at 8 Cottage Avenue in 'Sconset after having been moved several times since it was constructed around 1873. It was not uncommon during the 1800s to dismantle a building, transport it to a new location on the island, and reassemble it. (Photograph by Richard Trust.)

A group of thespians from the Actors Colony shares space on 'Sconset Beach in 1914. Pictured from left to right are Ben Wood, Peggy Westerton, William Courtleigh, Elizabeth Klenny, Robert Mackay, unidentified, Jack Hazzard, Frank Deacon, and Joe Kilgour.

The 'Sconset Actors Colony had among its clan numerous avid golfers, many of whom are pictured in this 1910s photograph, taken in front of the clubhouse at Siasconset Golf Course. This photograph came from the albums of Pauline Mackay, who won the United States Women's Amateur Golf Championship in 1905 at Oakley Country Club in Watertown, Mass. The clubhouse was recently reinvigorated by the Nantucket Islands Land Bank, which now owns and operates the public golf course.

The provenance of this photograph is unknown, but it shows mostly men, garbed in women's clothing; that's something of which Shakespeare might have approved. 'Sconset's penchant for theater is well documented, and these lads were probably posing during the production for a performance at the 'Sconset Casino. The fellow on the far left, wearing a straw hat and a watch fob, could be the show's director.

Active members of the Actors Colony gather in 1903 on the porch of Harry "Henry" Woodruff's cottage "Aloha" at 4 Morey Lane. Woodruff is in the center, surrounded by (clockwise from Woodruff) Henrietta Crossman, Nanette Comstock, Mary Shaw, Mrs. Digby Bell, Digby Bell, Walter Hale, Frank Burbeck, Frank Perry, and Robert McKay, a.k.a. Mackay.

The cast of *A Likely Story* and *Turn Him Out* performed in 'Sconset in 1889. Their names as written on the back of the photograph: J.M.T. Pope, J.C. Gray, R.C. Powell, A. Farquhar, Morrell, C.S. Mather, Farquhar, Hartly, B. Bispham, C.F. Pope, W. Chittenden, Hampton, and Chittenden.

In this c. 1910 image, a group of actors are relaxing at the Ocean View House Hotel. From left to right are Robert Hilliard, two unidentified people, Peggy Westerton (holding dog), two unidentified men, Robert Carter (with beret), Bijou Fernandez, Daniel Frohman (in rocker), and unidentified.

Actor and avid golfer Digby Bell (1849–1917) is teeing off at hole No. 7 on a sunny day around 1915 at Siasconset Golf Course. Digby and his second wife, Laura Joyce Bell, were highly acclaimed comic-opera singers who performed in the early days of the casino. Laura died in 1904 at age 46.

Henry Ingott "Harry" Woodruff (1869–1916) began performing at age nine with a role in *H.M.S. Pinafore*, so by the time he arrived in 'Sconset, in 1901, he was in his early 30s and quite comfortable as a member of the Actors Colony. He was so at ease that he had an upside-down home built at 4 Morey Lane. Named Aloha after Woodruff had admired the architectural style on a visit to Hawaii, the house had bedrooms on the first floor and an open living area on the second floor that provided residents and guests extraordinary views.

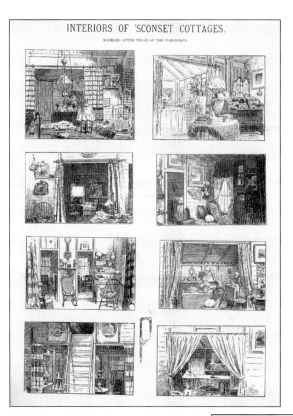

INTERIORS OF 'SCONSET COTTAGES.

MODELED AFTER THOSE OF THE FISHERMEN.

The interiors of eight 'Sconset cottages, which were modeled after the dwellings of the fishermen from the pamphlet *The Patchwork Village, 'Sconset by the Sea* by Edward F. Underhill.

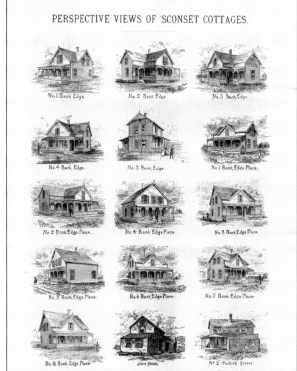

PERSPECTIVE VIEWS OF 'SCONSET COTTAGES.

These are drawings of 15 'Sconset cottages from the pamphlet *The Patchwork Village, 'Sconset by the Sea* by Edward F. Underhill. Among the cottages featured are Bank Edge, Bank Edge Place, and 2 Pochick Street.

Detroit-born but 'Sconset-driven, David Gray poured his heart but also his money into various causes in the village. For his contributions and his passion for America and its stars and stripes, Gray (1870–1928) was honored on July 4, 1929, with the placement of a flagpole in the center of the 'Sconset rotary. Along with a brass plaque, it remains in place to this day. (Photograph by Maurice W. Boyer, courtesy of Rob Benchley.)

This is actress Mary Shaw (1860–1929), described on the back of the photograph as an "old time actress and 'Sconset summer resident in one of her theatrical roles." An integral part of the 'Sconset Actors Colony in its early days, Shaw was from Boston, where she first appeared on stage in 1878. Her acting career endured for almost 50 years, although her last documented visit to 'Sconset was in 1905. She was a popular figure on Broadway in New York City, where her son Arthur (1881–1946) also enjoyed a run of successes.

Writer, theater critic, humorist, and actor Robert Benchley and his wife, Gertrude, are pictured in 'Sconset in the early 1940s. A native of Worcester, Massachusetts, Robert (1889–1945) first visited the little village in 1922 and quickly became enamored. While his work in New York City and Hollywood, California, kept him away from 'Sconset beyond his liking, other family members put down roots. That includes his son Robert Jr., whose primary income stemmed from the field of advertising, and grandson Robert Benchley III, journalist, photographer, and coauthor of this book.

Legendary entertainers Eddie Cantor and Sophie Tucker clown around on 'Sconset Beach in the 1930s. Both were popular with American audiences nationwide through their television appearances in the 1950s. Cantor (1892–1964), born in New York City, was a singer, songwriter, comedian, dancer, and actor who performed on Broadway and radio as well as TV. Ukraine-born Tucker (1886–1966) also starred on a variety of stages and, when in London for her 1934 Royal Command performance, greeted Britain's King George V with "Hiya, King."

Three

RIDING THE RAILS

With 'Sconset clearly a popular summer destination but still an uncomfortable, seven-mile horse-and-carriage ride from town over bumps, ruts, and other late-19th century annoyances, a railroad was a welcome mode of transportation from Nantucket town.

First, the narrow-gauge road of the Nantucket Railroad brought beach-seeking townies and mainland visitors to Surfside, on the island's south shore, beginning in the spring of 1881. It was deemed a success. An estimated 30,000 passengers seated in open-air cars paid the railroad's 35¢, roundtrip fare in that inaugural season, and Surfside appeared on the brink of boom-town status. Within two years, the newly placed Surfside Hotel was filling its rooms, and the Surfside Land Company had sold 180 lots.

'Sconset was not to be left behind, and in the summer of 1884, the little engines that could carried exhilarated passengers into the village of little cottages and fresh ocean breezes. 'Sconset was on its way to solidifying the foundation from which sprung today's alluring tourist destination.

Alas, the railroad beds were not paved with gold. By the mid-1890s, costly repairs and the washout of tracks amid south beach erosion from winter storms led to staggering financial losses. The Nantucket Railroad shut down but was reorganized and resurfaced as the Nantucket Central Railroad Company. The new entity continued running trains to 'Sconset, but Surfside was no longer a stop along the way. That left the Surfside Hotel without its main source of revenue and, before too long, was in disrepair. The land company, whose investors/speculators thought Surfside's future as a major tourist draw was virtually guaranteed, went belly-up.

Changes in the railroad's rolling stock were frequent. A used engine named the 'Sconset came into service in 1885, along with a 64-passenger closed car. Other cars came and went, keeping the flow of passengers intact, until increased accidents and more financial losses, coupled with several changes in ownership, led to the cessation of railroad service in 1917.

Automobiles were allowed on Nantucket in 1918, and in that same year, the Nantucket Railroad rails, two railroad cars, and engine No. 2 were shipped to Bordeaux, France, for use by the Allied Expeditionary Forces. The Allies prevailed; Germany was beaten back, and history has it that 'Sconset played its role in saving the world from a tyrannical force.

Tickets like this permitted riders of the Nantucket Railroad Company to travel with relative comfort the seven-mile distance from Nantucket town to 'Sconset, and back, starting in 1884. The first-year, round-trip fare when the train carried passengers only to Surfside and back was 35¢. The year was 1881. Rail service was extended to 'Sconset in 1884 and served until 1917.

Engine No. 2 of the Nantucket Railroad Company is pictured here with two passenger cars outside the railway's 'Sconset station around 1910. After continued loss of revenue and repeated derailments and other accidents, the railroad shut down in 1917. World War I ended in 1918, and the Nantucket Railroad Company contributed to the armistice by sending train tracks, engine No. 2, and two railcars to France for use by the Allied Expeditionary Forces in beating back the Germans.

A work crew is laying track for the Nantucket Railroad, which would begin carrying passengers to 'Sconset in 1884 after stops at Surfside and Tom Nevers. Four men are shown placing support beams for the railroad track, which was of the narrow, three-gauge variety.

Railroad cars are pictured coming by barge and going ashore at Commercial Wharf in waters off Nantucket town on May 29, 1910. A large crowd had gathered on the wharf to greet the newest members of the Nantucket Railroad's rolling stock.

Two railroad flagmen, actually a pair of barefoot boys, are holding a flag at the Orange Street railroad crossing in Nantucket town.

Capt. Jack Killen is shown here on June 22, 1909, among a group of highly interested onlookers driving a golden spike to connect the newly replaced rails near the terminal at 'Sconset.

In this c. 1915 photograph, a Nantucket Railroad Company train steams its way on Easy Street for the seven-mile trip to 'Sconset. In the boat basin behind the engine and tender and one passenger car are catboats, fishing boats, dories, and schooners.

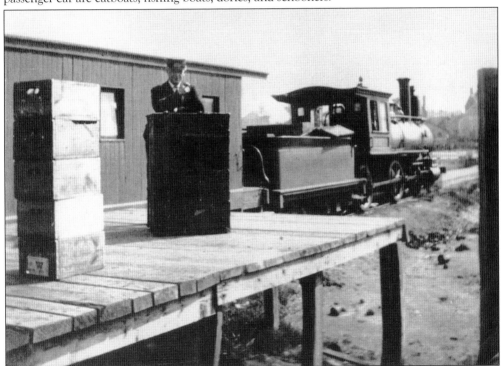

A railroad engine is at the loading dock on Easy Street in Nantucket town. The conductor is checking a summary of goods to travel as freight, some of which stand piled up on the platform prior to its trip to 'Sconset.

An early 1900s employee of the Nantucket Railroad stands in front of the door at the station on Steamboat Wharf in town. Railroad timetables are posted on the building to the left of the door.

Women played a major role in the Nantucket Railroad, as evidenced by this employee at the Steamboat Wharf station in Nantucket town. Like the photograph of the male employee on this page, this image was a gift of 'Sconset philanthropist David Gray.

Two Nantucket Railroad cars, the "Bird Cage," left, and the "Bug," are stopped at the head of North Wharf on Easy Street downtown prior to its trip to 'Sconset. Two women and two men are in the Bird Cage, while a boy stands next to the railroad operator.

An open-sided Nantucket Railroad car was captured on a glass-plate negative by an unidentified photographer during the 1890s. With the cessation of train service on Nantucket in 1917, an old railcar was abandoned but eventually saved and resurfaced as Allen's Lobster Grill and Diner on Main Street. Since 1977, it has been the Club Car, a popular seasonal restaurant and bar.

The Nantucket Railroad's venerable engine No. 2 is shown here around 1910, with two men on the left acknowledging the presence of the photographer. Engine No. 2, known as the " 'Sconset," was among the railroad's "hardware" sent to Bordeaux, France, in 1918, helping the Allied Expeditionary Forces defeat Germany.

This photograph depicts the Nantucket Railroad station downtown on Steamboat Wharf before a trip to 'Sconset. Two conductors will collect tickets as the ride gets underway.

A Nantucket Railroad train is pulling into the station in 'Sconset. Note that a stairway down from the South Bluff is in the foreground.

This 1890s scene has passengers standing by at the Nantucket Railroad train station for the trip back to Nantucket town. Note the expansive Ocean View House hotel looming in the background up on South Bluff.

This 1901 image from a classic glass-plate negative shows Nantucket Central Railroad's Engine No. 1 on Easy Street in Nantucket town. It is thought that the engine had just been delivered to the island.

The train to 'Sconset passed by the South Bluff of the village in this run just after the turn of the 20th century. Problems that beset railway transportation on Nantucket—washouts, derailments, equipment breakdowns—caused a merry-go-round of organizational shifts. It began as the Nantucket Railroad Company, its name from 1881 to 1894; it was the Nantucket Central Railroad from 1894 to 1909 and the Nantucket Railroad again from 1909 to its shutdown in 1917.

The first train to Sconset. July 22.1909

After the Nantucket Railroad Company reorganized as the Nantucket Central Railroad, this is the first train leaving Easy Street downtown for 'Sconset on July 22, 1909.

The second decade of the 20th century saw this image forming. It is a crowd gathering next to a train at the 'Sconset railway station, which can be spotted in the center of this photograph donated by philanthropist David Gray.

Another summer day, another trip—this one in 1905—finds a Nantucket Railroad train steaming into the 'Sconset station on the South Bluff.

This is a 1911 image of a railroad station at Steamboat Wharf in Nantucket town. As the sign indicates, passengers gathered there to catch the "Trains for Sconset," the absence of the apostrophe notwithstanding. Since 1917, the island's pretty little village on the edge of the sea has survived the absence of the Trains for 'Sconset.

Four

CODFISH PARK

Codfish Park is a gem in the crown of Nantucket Island, shining as notably as the rest of 'Sconset itself. And like the latter, "the Park" represents an example of successions and migrations, both by people and the very sand on which it sits.

Up until the early 1800s, it was only a narrow and unnamed strip of uninhabited beach under 'Sconset's coastal bank, as ordinary as any other beach around the island. But the tidal currents changed, the beach began widening, and it did so for the next 150 years or more. In those early days of accretion, the fishermen and their families who had built their first shacks up above the bank started building down on the beach; they were just getting their boats and their gear closer to the fish.

And fish they did. The waters off 'Sconset abounded in cod, a fish whose global importance is written in the history books. The early 'Sconset fishermen used baited hand-lines from their small three- and four-man boats in the 1700s; in the 1800s, they switched to one-man dories, a few relics of which can be seen in the photographs that appear on the pages to follow.

The American boom of tourism in the 1880s lifted Nantucket out of its previous economic slumps; 'Sconset benefited as well, and it would put Codfish Park, literally, on the map. Grand hotels, supper clubs, and intentionally quaint developments were built up on the bank; the people who did the work for the new visitors—the cooks, maids, and other "domestics"—occupied the old fishing shacks and thus created the new Codfish Park. The hotels came and went, but the legacy of the park remained intact with its global representation of African Americans, Bermudians, Portuguese, Azoreans, and Cape Verdeans.

Today, the ocean keeps nibbling away at the sands it once deposited, leaving an uncertain future of this little jewel.

The winding path in this 1880s photograph leads down the coastal bank to Codfish Park. It became known as "Hairpin Turn." Earlier in the century, the beach here was quite narrow, but through natural deposition, it widened by hundreds of feet, enabling the formation of a squatters' community of fishermen. Lumber for these shanties came from other dilapidated buildings and driftwood from wrecked ships.

From a stereograph taken in 1872 on the beach in Codfish Park, a group of islanders poses for the camera amid dories and other fishing paraphernalia. They were identified in 1912 by the *Inquirer and Mirror* as, from left to right, Cromwell Morselander, Alexander Paddack, Joseph Sheffield, Albert S. Clark (with an oar), Valentine Aldrich, Horace Hewitt, Valentine Holmes, Philip L. Holmes, Amelia Morris, Josephine Holmes, and George Wilber.

Later in the 1880s, the beach in front of 'Sconset continued to widen, and fishermen built more shanties below the bank. Along with haddock, cod was the primary catch in those days, and the best fishing was in the spring and the fall when most visitors to the village (including photographers) either had not arrived yet or had already gone home at the end of the summer.

Photography was relatively new to America in the mid-19th century; the photographer who recorded this image in Codfish Park probably used a tripod to steady his bulky wooden view camera, having lugged his sensitized glass plates down to the beach along with his leather cases and black hood. Or perhaps the nice man in the horse-drawn rig gave him a ride there. The fishing shacks are looking ramshackle, but that is the way they were built.

This aerial shows much of the village of 'Sconset, and all of Codfish Park. The view is looking northward (toward Cape Cod) at the very eastern edge of Nantucket Island. Of note in this 1926 view is the widening beach on the right-hand page, where "the Park" is nestled. The original fishermen's shacks up on the bluff were increasingly reoccupied by newcomers as 'Sconset's popularity exploded in the mid- to late-19th century; the fishermen moved "Down Bank," presumably closer

to the fish. At the time, the cod-fishing here was superb, and the product was hailed as some of the best in the region. By the mid-20th century, the cod had lost its prominence from over-fishing, and the shoreline seen here began its persistent retreat back through the streets of Codfish Park. The white "blip" at the top of the left-hand page is Sankaty Lighthouse (page 71), where erosion has also taken its toll. (Photograph attributed to Maurice W. Boyer, courtesy of Rob Benchley.)

The Nantucket Historical Association describes this half-stereograph as a "small shack in Siasconset, probably Codfish Park." Clues, including the period dress, date this photograph to the 1860s, which makes this a very early rendering of life "below the bank." It is possible that the main part of the building, on the left, was moved here from a different location: the shingle siding is quite weathered, possibly predating its existence in this location.

In the 1880s or 1890s, this unidentified fisherman posed for the camera along with his unmoving horse. The cart is known as a "dray," a kind of over-sized pull-cart that used a wooden barrel instead of a set of wheels, making for easier navigation in the soft sand. The tails of dried fish (probably cod) can be seen sticking out of the barrow.

This postcard depicts what was once a prolific industry (besides whaling) on Nantucket: cod-fishing. And in this aptly-named place, fishermen used baited handlines from their in-shore dories to catch fish by the thousands. Written accounts say that the 'Sconset cod was the best to be found on the market because it was salted and dried right near the beach. Salt for curing came from as far away as the Turks and Caicos Islands.

Henry S. Wyer posed a group of folks around a "fish-dray" below the bank at 'Sconset. Of interest in the background appears a splay of garbage sliding down the bank. Such tailings were noted in 1797 by John Spooner, who wrote that "all sectarian principles are viewed here (like the offals of the fish) as the refuse of the village. These are all cast down the bank together."

In the mid-1880s, vacationing families found their way to 'Sconset and the beach at Codfish Park. These kids are not so much dressed for swimming as they are for just enjoying their morning outing in a photograph taken in the early 1920s. Also not dressed for swimming is the person whose shiny shoes appear on the far left of this photograph. (Courtesy of Rob Benchley.)

The US Life-Saving Service, the precursor to the US Coast Guard, was established in 1878 to provide aid to those shipwrecked on all the coasts of the United States. Nantucket had its share of lifesaving stations then, and one of those was located on the beach at an area known as Coskata, about five miles north of 'Sconset. Here, in 1932, one of its members drives a modified Ford Model T beach buggy over the dunes in Codfish Park. Note that the photographer's composition was a bit astray, cutting off the top of the man's head. (Courtesy of Nelson K. Eldridge.)

Many shacks built in the 1800s and before were repurposed in later years. These unidentified men appear to be offering something from this converted shack. Possibly fried "chitterlings, tongues, and breeches," which were savored fare in those days, being the leftover parts of the codfish that were not shipped off-island. This shack became an ice-cream and hot dog stand in the 1920s and is a private home today.

On the beach at Codfish Park, would-be swimmers took in the sought-after soothings that were promoted by advertisers of 'Sconset and its charms. There is no sandbar to speak of at 'Sconset Beach, as strong tidal currents wash the shore hourly in potentially dangerous regularity. Early accounts of swimming here mention safety ropes that were strung at right angles to the shore. (Photograph by Gertrude Darling Benchley, courtesy of Rob Benchley.)

The beach cottage "Sandpiper," pictured here on a sunny morning, was once the home of George Rogers, a well-known 'Sconseter. His knowledge of fishing was admired by the community, as he taught many youngsters the "ways" of the art. This house appears in many early photographs of Codfish Park, but in 1992, after 100 years of existence, it was swept away during a fierce ocean storm. (Photograph by Rob Benchley.)

By the 1970s, the scene in Codfish Park began to change markedly, as older buildings were either torn down or made vastly larger. In the early 1990s, the ocean started to take back what it had laid down more than 100 years ago. In this January photograph, taken during the Blizzard of 1996, one of the old shacks can be seen floating off, while another house is left hanging over the dune. (Photograph by Rob Benchley.)

Five

SIASCONSET CASINO

The Siasconset Casino Association (SCA) was founded in 1899, and with $3,000 raised by SCA organizers, the casino was built, and it opened in July 1900. That gave 'Sconset residents and visitors an entertainment venue on New Street, in the heart of the village. Theatrical performances, sometimes with vacationing Broadway actors joining local thespians, were held at the casino. Before the casino was in place, such shows were staged at the 'Sconset railway station on the beach.

Masquerade balls, dances, wedding receptions, movies, lectures, fundraisers, bingo nights, and more have been featured through the years in the great hall. Despite the name "Casino," no gambling is conducted there—but tennis is. The casino opened with two tennis courts, four more were installed within the first decade, and today, eleven clay courts are there for the playing.

Considered a "community center" for the villagers, the casino is open each year from mid-May until the end of September. But while it is open, it is not unusual for a crowd of 200 to pack the hall for History Night, an annual presentation by the 'Sconset Trust.

"What's so unique about 'Sconset is that everybody is very plugged into the history of the community," said Dave Dunn, assistant to casino general manager Mike Coleman. "Any chance to further that history, to make sure it's not lost, to make sure it's preserved, I think the people recognize that, and that's why they turn out in full force for that type of event."

While most casino events have been deemed successful, two early ventures went by the wayside. The SCA erected a new building to accommodate two lanes of bowling and paid kids from the neighborhood to serve as pin boys. That was in 1909. By 1920, financially in the gutter, bowling was shut down. In 1912, the Pacific Bank opened a branch at the casino. But after one season, it, too, bit the dust.

The above photograph presents an overview of the 'Sconset Casino as seen from Main Street and Park Lane early in the 20th century. Pictured are the 'Sconset Union Chapel (far left), a former bowling alley (left center), the casino (center), tennis courts surrounding the building, and more than a dozen spectators watching a match in progress. Structural changes were required in the 1920s, with local philanthropists David and Martha Gray donating to the coffers. Outside walls and a weakened frame were reinforced, and doors and windows were added as part of the update. Below is the casino as it appeared in 2018. Countless changes have come about through the years, but one of the most dramatic outdoors is the increase in the number of tennis courts from 2 when the casino opened in 1900 to the 11 in play now. (Below photograph by Rob Benchley.)

From left to right, Henry "Harry" Woodruff, Maurice Campbell, Robert Mackay, and Frederick Perry are playing tennis around 1903, not at the casino but on the lawn of one of the Underhill cottages on the South Bluff of 'Sconset.

A young woman named Winifred Clark, all decked out in her tennis whites, appears more than ready to take on any challenge. The caption attached to the original photograph, snapped by Margaret Fawcett Barnes in the early 1900s, reinforces the notion of Clark's competitive nature. It reads, "Winifred Clark w.o.c. 'Oh you tennis player.'"

NANTUCKET
Guide to
HOTELS
RESTAURANTS
SIGHT-SEEING
ENTERTAINMENT
SHOPS•ROOMS
INFORMATION
CHURCHES
"Everything You
Need to Know"

WEEK OF
AUGUST 14, 1939

FLORA CAMPBELL
in "Accent on Youth" at 'Sconset
Casino Thurs., Fri. and Sunday.

Pictured here is the front cover of *This Week in Nantucket*, a guide to area sights and events, which, for the week of August 14, 1939, featured an appearance in *Accent on Youth* by actress Flora Campbell at the 'Sconset Casino. The guide provided information on hotels, restaurants, sightseeing, entertainment, shops, rooms, and churches.

John Wagley, left in the photograph below, rehearses for an unspecified role at the 'Sconset Casino during the 1950s. He is wearing a cardboard-box hat and carrying a fireplace broom. Performers in the background are unidentified. A native of Cleveland, Ohio, Wagley visited Nantucket and, as a child, celebrated his August birthday there every summer but one during World War II. "My mother was afraid the ferry would be torpedoed," he said in a July 2019 interview with coauthor Richard Trust, "so she sent me to a camp in New Hampshire. I told her to never do that again. She didn't."

Two people sitting on the grass are watching a silent film *The Sinners*, with Alice Brady of the Actors Colony in the cast, being shot in 1920 on a set adjacent to the 'Sconset Casino.

Popular fare at the casino included summer revues known as *On the Isle*, which began in the 1940s as a fundraiser. After a hiatus of 40 years, the program was revived and is now in its 20th year and counting. Pictured here in a 2005 musical production of *Up in the Rafters* are, from left to right, (first row) Jennifer Psaradelis and Michael Viano; (second row) Betsy Boe, Robin Hammer, John G. Lathrop, and Betsy Smith; (third row, among others unidentified) John McCarthy, Courtney Hudson, and Louise Strasenburgh. (Photograph by Rob Benchley.)

Two women are playing tennis at the 'Sconset Casino not long after the facility opened in 1900. Note that the woman at right is in the process of serving to her opponent in a sun-splashed game of doubles.

Helen Clark Farnum, second from right, is joined by a group of friends—all brandishing their tennis racquets—on one of the dutifully maintained courts at the 'Sconset Casino in 1922. While a student at Vassar College, Helen attended Frederick Howe's 'Sconset School of Opinion one summer. She also found time for some tennis.

Several tennis matches are being contested at the 'Sconset Casino in the 1930s as a large gathering pays rapt attention. While a number of today's players have memberships and may play at the casino at almost any daylight hour, non-members are permitted to reserve court time daily between 1:00 and 3:00 p.m.

Women appear to be of the Victorian era in their elegant, turn-of-the-century threads while watching tennis matches at the 'Sconset Casino in the early 1900s. But the times they would be a-changing. By the 1930s, women had joined the men in regularly wearing tennis shorts on tennis courts. As headlined in a Quincy, Massachusetts, newspaper in 1934, "Shorts favored by Quincy girls," with the subhead as, "Abbreviated Trousers for the Fair Ones Are Rule Rather Than Exception on Tennis Courts."

In this image from 1941, caddies are practicing their tee shots at Sankaty Head Golf Club in 'Sconset. The young men got to play a round of golf, or parts thereof, whenever they had time after their training and working at the Sankaty Head caddy camp.

Sankaty Head Golf Club, which opened in 1922, has the nation's last working caddy camp. Begun in the 1930s, some 60 campers spend parts, or all, of their summers learning the trade. Fred Miller (right), who grew up in South Braintree, Massachusetts, and now resides in the Bay State town of Hingham, was 15 years old when he spent July and August 1948 at the camp. Now in his 80s, Miller no longer plays golf but prances around a tennis court after a 2018 knee replacement and outplays foes 10 or more years younger. "Golf is a very difficult game," he said. "In tennis, you can blame all kinds of things. You can blame your opponent, your partner, the weather. But with golf, it's only you, the golf club, and a ball. You can blame only yourself." (Photograph by Richard Trust.)

Six

SANKATY HEAD LIGHTHOUSE

The light went on in 1850, and it still shines brightly. And it is on solid ground, away from the danger of toppling 100 feet down the north 'Sconset bluff and onto the beach below. In 2007, perched only 68 feet from the North Bluff's edge, the iconic white tower with a thick red stripe was moved 405 feet to the northwest so that it now stands 267 feet from the edge of the erosion-ravaged bluff and just off the fifth hole of Sankaty Head Golf Club.

Sankaty Head was the third, and final, lighthouse built on Nantucket—Brant Point (constructed in 1746) and Great Point (1784) are the others—but Sankaty is the only one left standing with its original construction materials. Its bricks and mortar have stood the test of time, and annual maintenance helps to keep its best face before the public.

A lighthouse was a necessary tool to warn approaching ships of dangerous shoals lurking offshore in the mid-19th century. Congress appropriated $12,000 in 1848 for construction of Sankaty Head Light. By comparison, $4 million was raised by the 'Sconset Trust for transporting the 500-ton, 70-foot-tall lighthouse from bluff-side to near the fifth hole of Sankaty Head Golf Club.

Several times a year, the 'Sconset Trust opens the lighthouse to the public. Lovers of the light climb 60 steps up a spiral staircase and 10 more up a ladder to the lantern house. An extra treat is that visitors are allowed out on the balcony and can enjoy unobstructed, 360-degree views of the Atlantic Ocean, the golf course, the village of Quidnet with Sesachacha Pond, and Siasconset.

In 1944, the US Coast Guard took over the upkeep of Sankaty Head Light, whose beams can be seen from 24 miles at sea. In 2007, ownership of the beacon was transferred through the Nantucket Historical Association to the 'Sconset Trust, which is charged with its preservation while the Coast Guard continues to maintain operation of the light tower.

Sixty feet tall at construction, the lighthouse grew to 70 feet with the addition of a new lantern deck in 1888. In 1950, a total of 100 years after its installation, the original Fresnel light in the tower was replaced and is a popular exhibit at the Nantucket Historical Association's Whaling Museum.

This early photograph of Sankaty Head Lighthouse shows how the station would have appeared when the light was first illuminated in 1850. The lamp was fueled by whale oil and required the keeper to trim its wicks four times each night. The Fresnel lens that cast the beam was the height of optical technology available at the time. The brick keeper's house shown in this 1870s photograph was torn down in 1887.

A family enjoys a picnic near Sankaty Head, around 1900. In the background stands the newer Victorian-style double keepers' house (built around 1888), along with livestock barns and outbuildings. Since its construction, the lighthouse has always been a strong attractant for ships at sea (which were warned, ironically, to "stay away") and for people on the land.

The grounds at Sankaty have always drawn visitors, where unobstructed views of the Atlantic, Nantucket Sound, and 'Sconset village are plentiful when the fog has not rolled in. The lighthouse's broad red stripe, seen in the background, serves (even today) as a day-marker visible from miles offshore. In this 1911 photograph, the women have paused for a drink of water from a hand pump.

The purpose of Sankaty Light was to warn ships of the formidable shoals around Nantucket and especially the fierce (and often deadly) sandbars off 'Sconset shores. Its placement probably saved many lives and cargoes in the area, where thousands of ships plied the then-early shipping lanes. The bones of this old schooner came ashore near Sankaty in the 1930s. (Photograph by Gertrude Darling Benchley, courtesy of Rob Benchley.)

In the late 1880s, Sankaty's visibility was improved by raising the focal plane of the beacon an additional 10 feet. This photograph shows the elevated lantern house as it appeared in 1893, along with the new Victorian-style dwelling that housed the keeper, the assistant keeper, and both keepers' families. The trestle building on the left served as a temporary beacon while the lighthouse was being renovated.

Augustin-Jean Fresnel is credited with the invention of the lens that now bears his name. His first lens was installed in a lighthouse off the coast of France in 1823; the invention revolutionized oceanic shipping and passenger travel worldwide. Sankaty's lens (pictured here) was removed from the lighthouse in 1950 and remains on display in the Nantucket Whaling Museum. (Photograph by Rob Benchley.)

Sankaty Head Lighthouse is pictured in 1949, at the north end of Baxter Road. The summer homes at left are typical examples of 'Sconset's development that began in the late 1800s. The Sankaty Head Golf Club links can be seen, with Nantucket Sound in the far distance. The high bluff facing 3,000 miles of the open Atlantic was an ideal spot to place a lighthouse.

Compared with the top photograph, much erosion has occurred through the years at Sankaty Head. In addition to half a dozen houses being moved away from the bluff along Baxter Road in the early 1990s, the cliff edge was nearing with every ocean storm. At the turn of the 21st century, the 'Sconset Trust, a local conservation group, started a plan that would save Sankaty for future generations. (Photograph by Rob Benchley.)

By the fall of 2007, the 'Sconset Trust had secured enough funds through an Island-wide appeal to lift the lighthouse and move it to safer ground. Crews from International Chimney, Inc., and Expert House Movers, Inc., performed the task. The move took 10 days, moving the light 405 feet from its original location. A year to the day later, the lighthouse was reopened to the public. (Photograph by Rob Benchley.)

A gull's-eye view halfway through the process shows the carriage that the movers built to lift and move the lighthouse. The carriage itself was pushed imperceptibly along steel rails using hydraulic rams. Its target destination can be seen in the upper right of the photograph in the form of a new concrete foundation. (Photograph by Rob Benchley.)

Seven

NATIVE SON

Nelson "Snooky" Eldridge's life has not been all work and no play. Having put time in on various jobs through most of his 80-plus years, and still answering the call part-time for those needing some quick-fix plumbing, Eldridge always found time to play while growing up in his native 'Sconset. He and his friends had plenty of fun and games to occupy themselves as seven-, eight-, and nine-year-olds, with a bit of mischief thrown in.

"There were enough of us where we'd play a lot of games in the street, like tag and kick the can, down in Pump Square," Eldridge said. It was good, clean fun—but then came the dark side.

"A bunch of us had the old clamp-on, steel roller skates and we used to go over to Shell Street, because that was the only one where the asphalt was smooth enough, and drive old lady Valerie Cushman right up a wall," Eldridge said. "She couldn't stand the noise from it, so we'd just go there and torment the hell out of her."

Valerie, whose cottage "Heart's Ease" is still standing but under new ownership, retaliated by chasing her tormentors with a broom. "That didn't faze us," Eldridge said. Neither did the police, whom the late Valerie would invariably summon.

Patrol officer Charlie Handy told her if she hit one of the kids, he'd have her in court. Under those circumstances, she held both her broom and her tongue. "She knew better," Eldridge said. "You didn't argue with a cop in those days." Snooky and his buds, then, had a pass to harass. "They figured we were just having a good time during daylight in the fall," he said of the police.

Eldridge's father, Kenneth, was also a native 'Sconseter and a police officer before he took a job with the water department and became its superintendent. Snooky was a firefighter for most of his adult life, rising to call deputy chief, running 'Sconset, and was a fill-in police officer for several years. He still works, now part-time five days a week as a plumber, employed by the son of the plumber he worked for while in high school. Indeed, it has not been all fun and games and tormenting Valerie Cushman.

Does the name Myrtle Eldridge (pictured above) ring a bell? She literally rang enough bells to earn her collection a place in the Guinness Book of World Records. When she got married on November 2, 1963, her husband, Snooky (pictured below), had his own business, delivering propane. To get away from the phone calls, she would often visit the dump after supper. One night, she brought home a bell, her first on the way to 9,638, and a certificate signifying a Guinness World Record. When the former Myrtle Bennett of Chester, West Virginia, died in August 2006 after 42 years and nine months of marriage, the total was 11,500 bells of glass, porcelain, and metal. They range in size from one bell off a steam locomotive to some as pierced earrings, and they came from yard sales, antique shops, gifts from friends, and more. Today, they grace three rooms in the Eldridge home, including one that had to be added on to accommodate all of them. (Both photographs by Rob Benchley.)

Three generations of Nantucket Firefighters pose for the camera: Nelson "Snooky" Eldridge (right) with his son Earl "Snip" Eldridge (left) and Elizabeth Eldridge (top) Earl's daughter. Dressed in their turn-out gear, these Eldridges stand in front of the 'Sconset Fire Station (formerly the 'Sconset School) with a restored 1937 American Lafrance fire engine. (Courtesy of Nelson Eldridge.)

Snooky Eldridge, on the left, tells a story in 2004 during a monthly fire drill of the 'Sconset Fire Department. With brother Gerald Eldridge (center) and Skip Vollans, these volunteers share about 140 years of combined experience in 'Sconset's fire service. The department was established in 1895; it was disbanded in 2016 when its members, who were all older than 65, were forced to retire. (Photograph by Rob Benchley.)

In addition to the combination gas station-auto repair shop adjacent to Gordon's Market (pictured above, in the 1950s), John Salvas (pictured below, inside the market, in the 1940s) also operated a taxi service and barbershop. If one of his customers was getting a haircut and a telephone call came in for a cab ride, Salvas would put down his barber tools, leave his customer in the chair, pick up and drop off his cab rider, then return to barbering and completion of the haircut. Snooky Eldridge never experienced that inconvenience, but his father, Kenneth (also a native 'Sconseter), did. Salvas was cutting Kenneth Eldridge's hair when a call for a cab came in. Sure enough, Salvas left to cater to his taxi customer. When the barber returned to his shop, Eldridge was gone. The next time they met up, Salvas said, "You owe me money," to which Eldridge replied, "No, I don't. You never finished the job!"

Aline Salvas Winslow and cousin Germaine Pominville sit outside the building that houses the barbershop and taxi service operated by John Salvas. The photograph was taken in the late 1940s or early 1950s.

This iconic sign at the gas station run by John Salvas was a humorous way to add some geographic perspective: "Fill Up Now! Last Service Area Before Spain." That is where one would be if they traveled directly east across the Atlantic Ocean.

A 1947 Winslow family portrait in 'Sconset features, from left to right, Gordon W. Winslow Sr., John Salvas, Aline Salvas Winslow, Michael Winslow, and Gordon W. Winslow Jr.

Heart's Ease is a rose-covered cottage at 14 Center Street in 'Sconset. That was the house in which Valerie Cushman resided when then-youthful Snooky Eldridge and his pals "tormented" her, as detailed on page 77 of this book.

John Salvas made an unusual entrance into 'Sconset. Born February 22, 1887, in St. Robert, Quebec, Salvas pedaled a bicycle across the state highway to 'Sconset in 1905 at age 18. He had heard of an opportunity for a barber in 'Sconset, and having learned the trade, he sought and succeeded in securing the position. After a long career in 'Sconset, Salvas moved to Florida and died in 1966 at the age of 78.

"As You Like It" was the name of this mansard-roofed home in the heart of 'Sconset. Today, the site is a public park, but it housed the Salvas family and "John the Barber's" business, which included sales of gasoline and haircuts. Known locally as being somewhat crusty, Salvas would cut men's hair "when he felt like it." He also rented bikes to the summer people.

This 1940s photograph shows the Salvas home on the left, and Tony's Market on the right, where once a gallon of gasoline cost the same as an ice-cream cone. There have been many incarnations of "the Market": Tony's, Gordon's, or just simply "the Market."

Another important market in 'Sconset was La Petite Cottage, sellers of "dry and fancy goods." Also available for purchase were the photographs of Henry S. Wyer, one of Nantucket's earliest premier photographers; historians assume that Wyer is the man pictured on the left. Many photographs in this book are attributed to him.

Eight

MERCHANTS AND MERCHANDISE

Mark Donato owned and operated the 'Sconset Market from Memorial Day to Labor Day for 36 years, so he knew he would miss it when he leased the iconic business to Rolf and Cindy Nelson starting in May 2018. While a sense of melancholy swept over Donato not long after he closed for the final time on September 4, 2017, he knew it was time to enter a new stage of his life. He loved running the market but had plans to play golf, help his wife, Beth English; run her business, currentVintage, in Nantucket; and someday campaign for a place on Nantucket's select board (formerly board of selectmen).

"Just chatting with customers, who are actually my friends, I realized that, 'Oh my gosh, I'm not going to see these people on a daily basis,' " said Donato, a Michigan native whose family moved to southern California when he was four years old.

Donato had only vague knowledge of Nantucket, and none of 'Sconset, when, in 1980, he was a self-professed "ski bum" in Sun Valley, Idaho, and came east with his future first wife, Pamela McKinstry. Having fallen in love with 'Sconset, he bought the market in 1982 from then-Procter and Gamble CEO Robert Shetterly.

With the market hardly a moneymaker the first few years, Donato also worked as a carpenter to help pay his bills. His customers lined up at the door for the 8:00 a.m. daily opening, precipitating a rush for blueberry muffins, croissants, and other morning delights baked in the rear of the market. By noon, the baked goods turned to brownies and the sensational 'Sconset Cookie, a meal-in-itself. That cookie—about five inches across and featuring chocolate chips, oatmeal, raisins, and walnuts—gave way to fresh, out-of-the-oven baguettes after 4:00 p.m. Door closes at 10:00 p.m., lights out.

"I'm a lucky guy," Donato said. "For 36 years, I liked my job. I liked coming to work, even though it was every single day and 16-hour days. I'd arrive whistling, open the door, smile, and say, 'Hi, come on in. How are you?' I miss being the greeter. Those are my friends, and I miss seeing them every day."

When Mark Donato took ownership of the 'Sconset Market in 1982, the $100,000 purchase price was sealed with a handshake and his promise to seller Robert Shetterly that he would be in it for the long haul. Thirty-six years of running the business certainly qualified as the "long haul." It was on a "pay me when you can" basis that Shetterly handed over the keys to the market. It was not long before the debt was paid in full. Donato did not often man the cash registers or put ice cream on cones. That was done by local teens or in larger part by young men and women from foreign countries. In the earliest years of the Donato administration, the market employed primarily kids from Ireland. For a later stretch of summers, it was predominantly Jamaicans. For the last decade or so, the market's workforce has consisted mostly of Eastern Europeans, primarily from Bulgaria, Romania, Lithuania, and a smattering from Ukraine and Slovenia. (Both photographs by Rob Benchley.)

From 1993 to 2017, Rolf and Cindy Nelson leased and operated the popular 'Sconset Café, booked solid for dinner from the time it opened each Memorial Day weekend in May until its September closing around Labor Day. But after more than two decades of pleasing patrons' palates, the Nelsons turned the business over to Alex Ulgenalp and picked up the reins of the 'Sconset Market just a handful of yards away. Rolf and Cindy have, however, continued to manage and operate the Bookstore liquor business adjacent to the café. "It's a dream come true," Cindy said of running the market, where she and Rolf both worked as teens in the 1980s. Said Rolf, "We were in the restaurant business for 24 years, and we were ready for a new challenge. I always thought that the market would be a challenge, and our taking it over would create continuity within the community without too much change for the community." Cindy and Rolf met when they were working at the 'Sconset Café, both at the age of 17. They eventually went their separate ways off to college, worked elsewhere around the country (and the world, in Rolf's case) before returning, marrying, having two sons, one liquor store, one café, and a market. (Photograph by Rob Benchley.)

Alex Ulgenalp was working his fourth summer at the 'Sconset Café in 2017 when, as a 26-year-old sous chef, he took over from Rolf Nelson as executive chef. Not bad for someone from Tarpon Springs, Florida, who had never heard of Nantucket—let alone 'Sconset—before stepping ashore in 2014. Former 'Sconset Café operators Rolf and Cindy Nelson "discovered" Ulgenalp at the Culinary Institute of America in Hyde Park, New York, the same learning center from which Rolf graduated. The institute was hosting a career fair when Ulgenalp met the Nelsons, who asked Alex to consider their café. "I jumped right in and fell in love with it," Alex said. As was the case under Nelson management, the little nine-table restaurant continues to sell out both evening settings from soon after opening in early June until its closing a week after Labor Day. (Both photographs by Richard Trust.)

Welch's Market came on the 'Sconset scene in the early 1900s. "Fancy groceries, meats, provisions, cigars and tobacco" were on the list of items he advertised. Located at Pump Square (see the cover photograph of this book), it also housed a Kodak store in the 1960s, and then dozens of seasonal 'Sconset workers. Most recently, it has been carefully restored into a suitable house. This image was captured in 1928. (Photograph by Liscum Diven, courtesy of Rob Benchley.)

None of 'Sconset's markets sold hay in bulk, as far as is known, but this load was certainly going somewhere down Main Street in the early 1900s. Judging from the strong shadow under the wagon, and the flag flying on Levi Coffin's porch, this may have been part of a Fourth of July celebration. Note the windmill on the left-hand side of the photograph; there were many of those in 'Sconset. A public water system was not installed until 1925.

Sconset Flag Pole blew over in storm 1940

A strong wind brought down the David Gray memorial flag pole in 1940. This uncredited photograph shows the 'Sconset Bookstore, center, and a little peek of the post office on the left. On the right is the Atlantic and Pacific grocery store, which, not so oddly, got its name from Nantucket's rich history in the business of whaling. 'Sconset's A&P did not last long, and today it is the home of Claudette's, a revered sandwich and catering business. The meatloaf sandwich is outstanding.

Along with the 'Sconset Market, the buildings pictured here are likely the most visited of any in 'Sconset. They are, from left, the post office (zip code 02564), Siasconset Bookstore liquor store, the 'Sconset Cafe, and Claudette's sandwich shop. (Photograph by Rob Benchley.)

The Summer House Inn stands out in 'Sconset's history of restaurants. It opened in the early 1900s as the Old 'Sconset Inn and, in the 1950s, became the Moby Dick Inn and Cottages under the leadership of Myra and Clem Reynolds. It later passed on to Bob and Elaine Wiley, whose employees through the years numbered in the hundreds. (Photograph by Rob Benchley.)

This is today's view of the pool compound at the Summer House, with its terrific view of the ocean. Here are hosted weddings and anniversary parties, as 'Sconset has become quite the destination for such celebrations. In the 1960s, a turkey sandwich on Portuguese bread cost about $2 at the pool; at the old Moby Dick, a full dinner of filet mignon, a baked potato, and a salad was about $9. (Photograph by Rob Benchley.)

This postcard shows the entrance to the Moby Dick Inn as it appeared in the late-1960s. Set along Ocean Avenue, it offered unfettered views of the Atlantic right across the street. It was originally owned by Clem Reynolds, who bought it in 1936 when it was known as the Old 'Sconset Inn, with the latter dating to 1911.

Before Clem Reynolds sold the business to the Wiley family in 1963 (the same extended family that ran the famous Chanticleer), he built a swimming pool for those guests who may not have wished to brave the strong currents of the ocean nearby. Bob and Elaine Wiley ran it as the Moby Dick Inn and Cottages until 1981. It would then become known, as it is today, as the Summer House.

Clem and Myra Reynolds opened a cocktail bar below the bank in what was originally the train station of the old Nantucket Railroad; that building became the original "Moby Dick," which burned down in the summer of 1956. Afterward, the lounge was relocated in the Old 'Sconset Inn, and the whole affair was conjoined to become the Moby Dick Inn. This photograph shows the handiwork of Myra Reynolds, whose gardening prowess was often noted in the *Inquirer and Mirror* newspaper.

This image from the 1930s is of the Morris Ice Cream Parlor, dispenser of the homemade variety, and the business was on New Street. Etta Morris, the proprietor of the parlor, lived on nearby King Street.

The Chanticleer Restaurant, above, which has become a gourmet dining oasis of international acclaim, began as a tea room and ice-cream parlor in the first decade of the 20th century. It was opened by stage actress Agnes Everett on New Street, where it is still located, across from the casino. Merging two small cottages to start with, it took on a wing in which ice-cream-making equipment was installed. Everett introduced the ice cream cone to 'Sconseters and those who would visit the Chanticleer (French for "rooster"). Below, the restaurant's iconic carousel horse and surrounding flowers were among many other features—dormered east wing, extended dining, rooms for guests, and overall expansion and frequent updating—marking the 58 years of Wiley family ownership that followed the first years of Agnes's reign.

The Chanticleer is still a summertime favorite after more than 100 years, and co-owner Susan Handy, pictured here, believes she has the answer for the restaurant's longevity. "One reason is that every time it has changed hands, it's remained in the possession of those people for so many years and it has a continuous theme to it for all those years," said Handy, who with fellow co-owner and executive chef Jeff Worster has opened the Chanticleer every summer since 2006. The Wiley family's 58 summers of operation preceded a 35-year period during which Jean-Charles Berruet of Brittany was at first chef and then owner before it was sold to Handy and Worster. (Photograph by Rob Benchley.)

Agnes Everett (1873–1959), shown here, could not have seen it coming, that the little tea room and ice-cream parlor she opened as the Chanticleer in the first decade of the 20th century would be thriving in the second decade of the 21st century. Tea and ice cream gave way to, well, let co-owner Susan Handy describe – or try to – the type of food on the menu: "I would say it's morphed into—and I hate to use 'New American' because it's an old term from the 1970s and '80s, but they're kind of talking about that again— modern American cuisine. I always have a hard time (labeling it), but it's the same cuisine you'll see in the best restaurants in Paris or London or Morocco. . . . We've been always calling it modern French, but I honestly don't know. It's just cuisine. It's a mixture of all [co-owner/executive chef Jeff Worster's] experiences traveling, in Asia, the Mediterranean, up into Europe. And also a lot of the cuisine of the West Coast, where we spent a lot of time early on. It's a mix of all that."

The Dine-A-Mite Tea Room, run by Gwendolyn Gouin across the street from where the 'Sconset Market is today, was built in the mid-1920s after the Phillips Building was destroyed by fire on October 29, 1924. After 1946, the Shoals restaurant and the Driftwood Inn occupied the location until Island Service Co. (offering hardware, paint, and more) bought it in 1952. Robert Shetterly purchased it in 1964, and within two years, it debuted as the Porch Restaurant and a coin-op laundry. Paul Bixby bought it in June 1977, and it opened as a pub before becoming the China Seas in 1979. Rob Mitchell (Mitchell Management) owned it in the early 1980s, but it never resurfaced as a commercial enterprise. It was sold as residential property, which it remains today.

Noted photographer Henry S. Wyer, who recorded many aspects of late 19th and early 20th century Nantucket life, captured this 'Sconset scene at 25 Broadway. It is the year 1895, and this is the 'Sconset Store. One sign says, "Kitchen-Ware Department."

This 1907 photograph details the Central Market on Broadway in 'Sconset. Employee Maria T. Holden Folger is at left; the male employee is unidentified, but he made deliveries in the horse-drawn carriage. Signs read, "Shawaukemmo Boiling spring water and Provisions and Groceries." The market served the village by making its items available at the store or by home delivery.

Pictured here is the Phillips Store, but the building that houses it started out in the 1880s as a residence known as the Anchorage, and the same Phillips (H.C. Phillips) had a grocery there as early as 1907, Phillips Grocery, Bakery and Market. Phillips died in 1918.

A chicken perambulator, known more simply as a portable chicken coop, was the brainchild of Roland Bunker Hussey, seen here posing with chickens. Hussey (1851–1923) was not all about poultry. He feathered his financial nest as editor and publisher of the *Inquirer and Mirror* newspaper (from 1887 to 1907), president of the Citizens Gas and Electric Co., and a director of the Pacific Bank. He also was a member of many local organizations.

Many 'Sconseters whose homes look out at a beach or the ocean own a private right of way to the sand for time to spend in the surf and under the sun. Some means of passage are a simple sandy path that might wend its way past stands of protected dune grasses. Some might be a simple set of wooden planks set snugly in a wall of compacted sand a la a ladder. Still, others might employ a solid, arbor-like entrance with a gate leading to a path down to a beach. The one shown here is on the North Bluff, just off the Bluff Walk stairway to the beach at Codfish Park. (Photograph by Rob Benchley.)

Nine

NATIVE DAUGHTER

Bevin Bixby never ceases to feel fortunate that she is a native of 'Sconset and still lives the life of "an island girl." She knows many people who feel lucky that they visit every year, and she cannot blame them.

"Growing up here, I feel even more lucky that I get to call this home," Bixby said. "And it's been home my whole life. You don't realize how lucky you are. It wasn't until I went away to college and came back that I got to understand better what all the tourists were excited about."

Bixby was allowed to ride her bicycle alone, fearlessly, anywhere she wanted to from the time she was seven years old.

"My parents would tell me, 'Don't go in the ocean by yourself, don't go on the main street by yourself, wear your whites for tennis,'" she said. "Other than that, I didn't have a lot of restrictions."

Bevin's parents, Paul and Jacquie Bixby, own the property housing the Bookstore liquor store and the 'Sconset Cafe and lease it to those who manage and operate those businesses.

In her 30s now, Bevin still loves driving down Milestone Road under the canopy of trees, a sure sign that the whole town is right there, waiting.

"It's so picturesque, incredibly more beautiful than any picture book of Nantucket could ever be," Bixby said, "and has so many memories for me, from Daffodil Days where we used to climb out on top of the porch on the overhang of the liquor store and have the best view of the parade coming from town. As a little girl, I'd be watching people with their wedding gowns going to and from the beautiful chapel. And the beach is right there, and you have the absolutely beautiful homes and the rose-covered cottages. It's all so special, I don't know another word to describe it."

Then she laughs and says, "And it smells beautiful. To me, it's the combination of the roses and the salt air mixed with a little bit of the 'Sconset Market blueberry muffins. That whole scent is home, for me."

The Bixby family poses for a holiday photograph in 1993, a decade after they bought the Siasconset Bookstore, seen in the background. Pictured from left to right are (first row) a young Bevin and her brother Colin; (second row) Paul, Amanda, and Jacquie. Bevin is a woman for all seasons, saying, "We get the daffodils in the springtime that let us know summer is coming. You get the roses in July, and when autumn comes, the leaves are falling, and that's beautiful, too. Winter brings snow. I love a good snowstorm and walking around 'Sconset before any of it is shoveled away or any of the cars get out there. To see those normally rose-covered cottages covered in snow is really special, a side of 'Sconset that a lot of people don't get to see. And just when I think I'm done with a season, the next one begins. It's kind of perfect." (Courtesy of the Bixby family.)

Bevin Bixby is like most native 'Sconseters when it comes to preserving the village in perpetuity. She said she "appreciates the many people and organizations that came before me, and I recognize how special 'Sconset is. 'Sconset is 'Sconset and should always be," Bixby said. "We are trying to preserve the sanctity of the village. I don't have any children of my own, but I have two nephews who I'd love to see get to experience it the same way my siblings (Amanda and Colin) and I did." Bixby devoured the experience. She played tennis at the casino, ran around the Codfish Park playground that got washed away in a storm, and ate blueberry muffins at the 'Sconset Market. "Even as an adult," she said, "I still love those blueberry muffins." (Photograph by Rob Benchley.)

A favorite destination of many 'Sconset residents and visitors outside of the village is Altar Rock, located in the central moors. It is reputed to be the highest point on Nantucket (it is not), where commanding views of the island may be had if one knows where to look. The boulder, seen in this 1932 photograph, bears a plaque commemorating Henry Coffin (1807–1900), who was an early island landowner and benefactor. (Courtesy of Rob Benchley.)

This cartoon lampoons Nantucket's 18th-century ways as it encountered the 20th with an island-wide ban on automobiles (see page 21.) It accompanied Edouard Stackpole's piece for Automobile Quarterly in 1977, titled "Nantucket Versus the Chug-Buggy." Stackpole (1903–1993) was an ardent island historian, author, and newspaper editor, whose article about 'Sconset's lighthouse, "The Saga of Sankaty," is considered one of the most authoritative in print.

Ten

'Sconset Has Been Found

One of the fascinating aspects of 'Sconset while strolling about the village is reading the names of houses carved into or painted on the quarterboards, which most frequently are placed above, or at least near, the front doors of houses so adorned

The white cottage named "Svargaloka" (Sanskrit for "land of paradise") on Elbow Lane is seen by many passersby who either cross over Gully Bridge from Ocean Avenue on their way to Post Office Square or come into the square from one of the many side streets or down Milestone Road to Main Street.

Many of those who name their homes do so with humor and double meaning, bringing a smile to the observer. Bowing to the seasonal nature of 'Sconset—and of Nantucket, in general—a rose-covered cottage on New Street is named "Seldom Inn." Owing to its occupancy by the ocean is "Sea It Now." Another with the beach in mind, and in sight, is "It's View to Me." Plenty of 'Sconset houses are surrounded by tall privet hedges that provide lots of privacy; one is "Hedged In," and another, "Hedged About." The quarterboard on a plastic surgeon's residence reads, "Nippontucket," a nod to the nips and tucks of his profession.

People tend to relax in 'Sconset; some take it easy in "Takitezie" and others throw their cares away in "Why Worry." Some 'Sconseters in Codfish Park have "Gone Native," some have "Gone Crazy" in a cottage that appears to have been built partially underground. Then there is what some might consider the granddaddy of all quarterboard names, honoring a Sachem of Nantucket long since passed. The name on the 'board is "Wanackmamack," a tribute to one of two Native American chiefs who sold much of Nantucket to Thomas Mayhew and his son Thomas Jr. in 1659.

If quarterboards are only half the fun, then take a full measure of daffodils, such as a million-plus of those yellow beauties that blossom into Nantucket's Daffodil Festival annually on the last weekend in April. That alone is enough to make mid-spring come alive. Combine that with a Bluff Walk, and it is a 'Sconset "daily double."

A native of Hanover, Massachusetts, Jean Petty, left, spent time in the Bay State town of Scituate and in California before she opened and operated Nantucket Carving & Folk Art on Orange Street in 2007. There, with Paul McCarthy her main carving companion until the business closed in early 2019, she utilized her background as an artist and graphic illustrator and finished the quarterboards cut and chiseled by McCarthy. Jean opened Petty Folk Art & Carving in 2020 at 7C Hanabea Lane, Nantucket. (Photograph by Richard Trust.)

Paul McCarthy had nearly a half-century of woodcarving experience on his resume, working a dozen years with Jean Petty in her Nantucket Carving & Folk Art workshop that specialized in quarterboards showcasing the names of houses in 'Sconset such as "Seldom Inn," "Svargaloka," and "Sea it Now." It was said that when a customer good-naturedly referred to the veteran woodcarver as Paul McCartney, one retort was, "Paul McCarthy can't sing, but, then again, Paul McCartney can't carve." (Photograph by Richard Trust.)

The Elbow Lane cottage "Svargaloka" arrived, literally, in 'Sconset in the 1870s. It had been built originally on Charles Folger's farm west of Nantucket town, eight miles away. In 1860, an arson fire destroyed his barn (and most of his livestock), and the house was eventually split in two and moved to 'Sconset. House movings are frequent occurrences on Nantucket; the raw materials are scarce, and anything that can be reused, usually is.

Svargaloka's quarterboard got a fresh coat of paint before this modern photograph was taken. The arched arbor seen here replaced the added veranda seen in the 1880s photograph at the top of the page. The name itself comes from a Sanskrit word meaning "land of paradise," so-named by Ava Channing, whose extended family owned the house until 1930. (Photograph by Rob Benchley.)

The custom of attaching a quarterboard goes back 200 years or more, when people scavenged the signs off the beaches after Nantucket's many shipwrecks (see such an example on Page 15.) In time, the names became more reflective of the houses themselves, as well as their occupants. Moved from the edge of the bank after the "October Gale" of 1841, Seldom Inn became an adjunct to the Chanticleer Inn and is now owned privately. (Photograph by Rob Benchley.)

During its interesting history, Seldom Inn had been the home of Phebe Ann Coffin Hanaford (1828–1921). Born on Nantucket, she grew up in a Quaker household and taught at the 'Sconset School from 1846 through 1849. Hanaford left the island, married, and eventually became a Universalist minister—one of this country's first women to be ordained. (Photograph by Rob Benchley.)

Wanackmamack was a tribal chief, or sachem, who took part in many mid-1600s transactions that turned over large tracts of Nantucket land to the first wave of English settlers. That wave became a tsunami as the Wampanoag population withered from an estimated high of 3,000 on the island to zero with the 1855 passing of Dorcas Honorable; she was the last living Nantucket Wampanoag. (Photograph by Rob Benchley.)

The rose-covered cottage shown here is the Wanackmamack, whose quarterboard is pictured in the photograph at the top of this page. Many disputes over land traded or sold by Nantucket's Native Americans to the encroaching English settlers ended up as court cases. Contented with their early deals, the island's original residents grew increasingly cautious when considering further negotiations.

This is the second wireless telegraph station in 'Sconset, and those who manned the operation there were busy transmitting and receiving alerts about ships at sea that were in distress. This station played an enormous role in disseminating information after the *Titanic* struck an iceberg in the North Atlantic Ocean on the night of April 14, 1912. It was the first to receive distress signals from the lavish British vessel, which was thought to be unsinkable. One of the employees of the station, which was discontinued in 1922, was David Sarnoff, future president of the Radio Corporation of America (RCA). The 'Sconset station was run by the *New York Herald* for two years before it was sold to the Marconi Wireless Telegraph Company of America.

Springtime is a long way off in this late April photograph along Pitman Road in 'Sconset, where there is not a bud in sight. The field, barns, and farmhouse were part of the 1880s landscape north of the village during the period when 'Sconset experienced its biggest expansion to the south with grand hotels, "quaint" developments, and a railroad connecting stylish visitors with the steam-powered ferries that eventually went as far as New York City. As with all of the photographs in this book, none is older than 1865, when photography was just beginning to make its mark on the American scene. Had the camera been around just 30 years earlier, we might be able to see photographs of the construction of Sankaty Head Light (1850) or the Great Fire of 1846 that ruined most of downtown Nantucket and changed the island's course forever. The photograph here was taken in 2005, despite its older appearance. Today, the big barn seen in the background has collapsed, and the smaller one is ready to. Also, a new house occupies the open field. 'Sconset changes quickly in some areas, but not so much in others. (Photograph by Rob Benchley.)

The village had horses, houses, stores, and hotels, but the people of 'Sconset needed a proper place of prayer. That need was met in 1883 with the opening of the Gothic Revival–style Siasconset Union Chapel, which, now as then, is open to all faiths. The story began August 14, 1882, when 15 men formed a corporation and a board of trustees with the dual objective of finding a location for a house of worship and then a builder. The objective was met when Trustee Horatio Brooks donated a lot on New Street, and Charles W. Robinson and Dr. Franklin A. Ellis were hired as builders for $1,680. Various repairs and alterations have been required through the years, but the chapel remains an important center for community events both social and spiritual.

This is a contemporary view of the Siasconset Union Chapel, where weddings, musical programs, lectures, and Sunday and memorial services are among the events that take place in summer only. The chapel also features a Columbarium and Memorial Gardens, serving those who choose to have their ashen remains placed in urns for interment in permanently sealed niches. (Photograph by Rob Benchley.)

Having fun was the highest priority of the members of the Srail Club. Srail is Liars spelled backward, and the club was formed in 1930 by the Hon. Lee Parsons Davis, a New York Supreme Court Justice. Comprising island residents and men visiting for the summer, the club members gathered several times a week in the name of friendship and, above all, to tell tall tales. Their meeting place was on New Street in 'Sconset, in the ice house of Horace Jernegan's father. In that "clubhouse" was a brass sign that read, "SRAIL CLUB. YSAE OT TRUH. DRAH OT LAEH." Reverse the letters, and it is "LIARS CLUB. EASY TO HURT. HARD TO HEAL." Pictured above are club members on a float from the 1938 Fourth of July parade in Nantucket town. Dressed as old seamen, members are in a boat in the back of a flatbed Chevy pickup truck. The club was already disbanded when Justice Davis died in 1961.

Thanks to the contributions of 160 Nantucket citizens, in 1776, the well for the 'Sconset Town Pump was dug at a cost of 20 pounds, 4 shillings, and 9 pence. Water was greatly needed for the horses that transported people from town to 'Sconset, to clean and dress the catch of the seasonal fishermen, and to hydrate the sheep herds important to the economy of the day. It served the community for more than a century. It was rebuilt in 1882 and was in use until early in the 20th century. This is a photograph of the pump as it is today. (Photograph by Rob Benchley.)

On almost every corner in 'Sconset stands a relic of one kind or another, rich in the history of its very existence. Here on the corner of New and School Streets, the recent 'Sconset schoolhouse now houses the village's volunteer fire department, a near-relic itself now from budget cutbacks and other curious machinations of the modern world. It was built in 1917 for $7,000, but it shut its doors to students 46 years later as 'Sconset's year-round population declined. Buses would later provide transport for 'Sconset's children to the established schools farther inland. In the background of this photograph is the 'Sconset water tower, a gravity-assisted storage tank of 178,000 gallons, that would replace the 1776 well seen on the previous page. The cast-iron standpipe, built in 1925, helped quench the thirsts of 'Sconseters and the burgeoning throng of people who would surge to the island. The building pictured here replaced the original prairie-style schoolhouse shown on the next page. (Photograph by Rob Benchley.)

The old 'Sconset schoolhouse, built in 1843 and pictured above in the 1890s, contained one room in a building that by the second decade of the 20th century was deemed "not fitted for the needs of 'Sconset," from an article published September 23, 1916, in Nantucket's *Inquirer and Mirror* newspaper. After 73 years, the building was described as "old, uncomfortable, poorly lighted, unsanitary, and not large enough" to serve the community's children. Hence, the new school that debuted in 1917.

In this c. 1900 photograph, 10 of 'Sconset's little angels posed for a portrait in front of what was then called "the school-house on the hill." In 1870, a total of 50 children were enrolled, all of them—and one teacher—crammed into the small building. The image evokes reminiscences of a Laura Ingalls Wilder story, as 'Sconset was very much a kind of prairie town at the time. Although the building was eventually condemned, it was recycled and now is part of a local electrician's workshop.

Horace Jernegan, above, delivered ice to homes in 'Sconset during the Depression-era 1930s. The icehouse was on New Street, near the Chanticleer restaurant, and across the street from the Siasconset Casino. During the economically depressed times, work continued to be available in farming and other industries. In that period, 'Sconset and other Nantucket communities were served by local farms and dairies.

Nobel Prize–winning author John Steinbeck first visited 'Sconset in the summer of 1951, staying three months with his wife, Elaine, and sons, Thom and John, in the North Bluff cottage Footlight (pictured in a 1937 photograph, above, first house on left in foreground with steps protruding from a porch). Steinbeck (1902–1968) wrote a good portion of his novel *East of Eden* during this visit. The house afforded a view of the Atlantic Ocean at left and the view here is looking southward down Baxter Road. Due to erosion, the house was moved across the street in 1987. In the photograph at left, Steinbeck returned to 'Sconset in 1964 to celebrate Memorial Day and visit friends. Here at the beach, he and his wife hosted a small gathering where the fare included Portuguese bread, cheese pate, sweet vermouth, and Bellows Club bourbon—on the rocks. Shown here, the author has donned the carapace of a giant horseshoe crab for extra sun protection. (Both photographs courtesy of Rob Benchley.)

Herman Melville

Moby-Dick is considered among the greatest novels in American literature, but only 3,215 copies of author Herman Melville's classic-in-waiting were sold during his life. Because Melville's previous five books were slow to sell, only 500 copies were printed by publisher L. Richard Bentley when, on October 18, 1851, it was released in England as three volumes with *The Whale* as its title. Only 300 copies sold in four months. By the time the book was published in one volume in the United States by Harper & Brothers on November 14, 1851, Melville had changed the title to *Moby-Dick*. Harper's printed 2,951 copies, an estimated 1,500 of which sold in 11 days. Then sales dipped to less than 300 in 1852. Melville was born in New York City in 1819 and died in 1891, but it was not until the 1920s that scholars rediscovered *Moby-Dick* and its 135 chapters and 600-plus pages—and declared it a literary masterpiece. Melville visited Sankaty Head in 'Sconset in 1852. This photograph was taken in 1861. (Photograph by Rodney Dewey, courtesy of the Library of Congress.)

Outside of his own household, Peter Benchley was hardly a household name when he wrote a little novel about a fish—a big fish known as a great white shark. The novel—about a great white terrorizing a New England beach resort town—was not so little after all; it was titled *Jaws*, and suddenly this somewhat obscure freelance writer from New York City who followed family tradition of spending lots of time in 'Sconset struck it big-time after its publication by Doubleday in early 1974. Benchley's first novel, the hardcover edition remained 44 weeks on the *New York Times* bestseller list. The paperback published by Bantam followed, and it sold copies into the millions in 1975. That same year, the movie version of *Jaws*, directed by Steven Spielberg, hit theaters and became the highest-grossing film ever until overtaken by *Star Wars* two years later. Three *Jaws* movie sequels followed, and the book has sold 20 million copies worldwide. When Peter Benchley died in 2006, not long before his 66th birthday, he and his book were indeed household names in countless households. (Photograph by Beverly Hall.)

Walter Folger, pictured at right in his US Coast Guard uniform, was a 'Sconset native who died September 21, 2017, at age 93. He was a Merchant Mariner in World War II and helped deliver supplies by ship to the Soviet Union while his convoy was under fire by German submarines. Walter and his wife, Veronica, had four children and three grandkids; Veronica died in 2012. Walter joined the Coast Guard after his marriage in 1951 and retired to 'Sconset in 1978 with the rank of captain. He was born into an iconic Nantucket family, dating to the founding-father Folgers. Abiah Folger (1667–1752) married Boston soap maker Josiah Franklin, and bore a son, Benjamin Franklin. Yes, that Benjamin Franklin. And, if you believe the best part of waking up is Folgers in your cup, thank James A. Folger (1835–1889). J.A. founded the Folgers coffee company. Below, photographed at Codfish Park in 1926, are, from left to right, (first row) Ruth Dennis Folger, Walter's late oldest sister; Bette Flannery, a cousin; and Walter, at two years of age.; (second row) Ruth Tangney, Walter's maternal grandmother; Carl Bishop, a family friend; and Lila Folger, Walter's mother. (Both photographs courtesy of the Folger family.)

The Treasure Chest was a gift shop at left on Elbow Lane, just off the 90-foot-long wooden Gully Footbridge that was built (in a flimsier version) by developer Charles H. Robinson in the late 19th century. The sign visible in this 1930s image reads, "Unusual Gifts, Wearing Apparel, and Lending Library." The building was destroyed by fire on April 7, 1985, and at that time, it was no longer a gift shop or beauty parlor but, as it is today, after it was leveled and reconstructed, a private home and rental property.

The iconic sundial on the wall of the former Treasure Chest, seen close-up, is still in use today. Note, however, that the words over the wall clock, "Treasure Chest of sunny hours," are no longer there in today's version (see page 121.)

The Gully Footbridge covered in snow is a sight rarely seen by most off-islanders. The majority of tourists flock to 'Sconset in the summer season, when about 2,000 people take up temporary residency. The 200 or so year-round 'Sconseters are "the lucky ones" who do get to experience the full range of weather conditions, the snow-covered landscape included. (Photograph by Rob Benchley.)

The full length and breadth of the Gully Footbridge, which connects the Ocean Avenue side of 'Sconset with Elbow Lane by spanning Gully Road below, can be appreciated in this photograph. On any given summer day, the bridge is a popular crossover for picture-takers, baby strollers, dog walkers, bicycle walkers, and ice-cream-cone aficionados. (Photograph by Rob Benchley.)

Daffodil Festival celebrants take part in the annual antique auto parade, which begins in Nantucket town and snakes its way seven miles to 'Sconset. There a tailgate picnic commences, with numerous tables set in place along Milestone Road and festival-goers consuming a vast variety of food and drink. Begun in 1975, the festival is held annually on the last weekend in April, and the auto parade is featured on that Saturday. People dress in daffodil-themed regalia, and more than a million of

the hardy yellow flowers have burst from their bulbs. Daffodil weekend enthusiasts pictured here on Milestone Road and headed toward the village are packed into a 1927 LaFrance ladder truck. From left to right in front are former Nantucket state representative Tim Madden; driver Rob Ranney; Ranney's late father, Flint Ranney; and Bert Johnson. (Photograph by Rob Benchley.)

Daffodils reign supreme annually on Nantucket, and those fortunate enough to be in 'Sconset for the Daffodil Festival and tailgate celebration are apt to repeat the trip and return the next year, the year after that, and so on. (Photograph by Richard Trust.)

On the weekends they are celebrated in Nantucket town and in 'Sconset, daffodils can be found almost anywhere as adornments: on the front, rear end, and hub caps of an automobile; on the outside boards of an old wooden barn; bunched together as a lovely bouquet; or as in the photograph above, a striking addition to sun hats. (Photograph by Rob Benchley.)

The Bluff Walk is considered one of the must-see, must-do attractions in 'Sconset. Created in the late 1800s, it was the brainchild of North Bluff home developer William J. Flagg. He wrote into the deeds of the stately homes he was constructing that a public right-of-way in the form of a pathway between the edge of the bluff and the line of homes would be in place. With the homeowners' compliance, the Bluff Walk became an instant site of passage for both residents and visitors who, when it was introduced, could walk all the way to Sankaty Head Lighthouse—a distance of 1.8 miles. (Photograph by Rob Benchley.)

Erosion through the years has cut into the bluff and necessitated the 2007 move of the lighthouse to safer ground 267 feet from bluff's edge. As of December 2018, the path was a little less than a mile in length, at 5,215 feet, from its start off Front Street to its end two houses shy of Bayberry Lane. It is open to foot traffic daily from sunrise to sunset year-round. (Photograph by Rob Benchley.)

Residents of high-end homes on Baxter Road take pride in their property anyway, but when they know that a steady stream of strangers strolls past their front yards, they make certain that all is in order and not a blade of grass is out of place. Clearly, some who play an "A" game add a humorous touch, such as the little creature riding his bike in this scene. (Photograph by Richard Trust.)

The bluff walk's tunnel of trees and shrubs frames a couple heading home after strolling the path and enjoying the view of Baxter Road homes on one side and the blue Atlantic on the other. Looking both ways certainly takes on a whole new meaning in this glorious slice of an enchanted Nantucket village known as 'Sconset. (Photograph by Richard Trust.)

DISCOVER THOUSANDS OF LOCAL HISTORY BOOKS FEATURING MILLIONS OF VINTAGE IMAGES

Arcadia Publishing, the leading local history publisher in the United States, is committed to making history accessible and meaningful through publishing books that celebrate and preserve the heritage of America's people and places.

Find more books like this at
www.arcadiapublishing.com

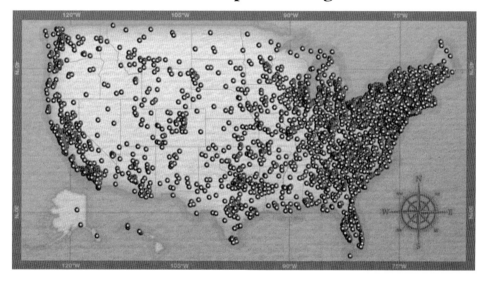

Search for your hometown history, your old stomping grounds, and even your favorite sports team.

Consistent with our mission to preserve history on a local level, this book was printed in South Carolina on American-made paper and manufactured entirely in the United States. Products carrying the accredited Forest Stewardship Council (FSC) label are printed on 100 percent FSC-certified paper.

MADE IN THE USA